By Jack Gantos

hole in my life

Jack Gantos

hole in my life

Farrar, Straus and Giroux
New York

Library of Congress Cataloging-in-Publication Data
Gantos, Jack.
    Hole in my life / Jack Gantos.— 1st ed.
    p. cm.
    Summary: The author relates how, as a young adult, he became a drug user and
smuggler, was arrested, did time in prison, and eventually got out and went to
college, all the while hoping to become a writer.
    ISBN 0-374-39988-3
    1. Gantos, Jack. 2. Authors, American—20th century—Biography.
3. Ex-convicts—United States—Biography. [1. Gantos, Jack. 2. Authors, American.
3. Criminals. 4. Authorship.] I. Title.

PS3557.A5197 Z468 2002
813'.54—dc21
[B]

                                                                2001040957

Excerpt from *On the Road* by Jack Kerouac, copyright © 1955, 1957 by Jack Kerouac;
reprinted by permission of Sterling Lord Literistic, Inc. Excerpt from *Revolutionary
Road* by Richard Yates, copyright © 1961, renewed 1989 by Richard Yates; reprinted
by permission of the Estate of Richard Yates.

I have learned this:
it is not what one does that is wrong,
but what one becomes
as a consequence of it.

— Oscar Wilde

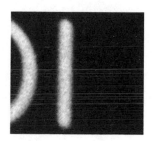

1 / look straight ahead

The prisoner in the photograph is me. The ID number is mine. The photo was taken in 1972 at the medium-security Federal Correctional Institution in Ashland, Kentucky. I was twenty-one years old and had been locked up for a year already—the bleakest year of my life—and I had more time ahead of me.

At the time this picture was taken I weighed 125 pounds. When I look at my face in the photo I see nothing but the pocked mask I was hiding behind. I parted my hair down the middle and grew a mustache in order to look older and tougher, and with the greasy prison diet (salted chicken gizzards in a larded gravy, chicken wings with oily cheese sauce, deep-fried chicken necks), and the stress, and the troubled dreams of capture and release, there was no controlling the acne. I was overmatched.

I might have been slight—but I was smart and cagey. I managed to avoid a lot of trouble because I knew how to blend in and generally sift through the days unnoticed by men who spent the majority of their time looking to inflict pain on others. I called these men "skulls" and they were freaks for violence. Here we were, all of us living in constant, pissy misery, and instead of trying to feel more human, more free and unchained in their hearts by simply respecting one another and getting along, many of the men found cruel and menacing ways to make each day a walk through a tunnel of fear for others.

Fear of being a target of irrational violence haunted me day and night. The constant tempo of that violence pulsed throughout my body and made me feel small, and weak, and cowardly. But no matter how big you were, there was no preventing the brutality. I had seen the results of violence so often—with guys hauling off and smashing someone's face with their fists or with a metal tool, a baseball bat, a rock—and all for no other reason than some imagined offense or to establish a reputation for savagery. When I lived and worked in the prison hospital—especially after I had become the X-ray technician—I was part of an emergency medical response team. I was called on day and night to X-ray all types of ugly wounds to see if the bones behind the bruised or bleeding flesh had been cracked, chipped, or broken. As we examined them, the patients would be telling the guards, "I didn't even know the guy" or (my greatest fear) "I never heard 'em, never saw 'em."

It was this lottery of violence that haunted me. Your number could come up anywhere, anytime—in the dark of night while you slept in a dormitory with a hundred other men, or in full daylight on the exercise field while you strolled in the sun. Once, in the cafeteria line, standing directly next to a guard, I watched a skinny black kid stab some other "blood" with a dinner fork. He drove it into the guy's collarbone so deep the doctor had to remove it with a pair of surgical pliers. AIDS wasn't a factor then. The blood that sprayed over the food trays was wiped off by the line workers and they kept spooning up our chow.

I wasn't raised around this level of violence. I wasn't prepared for it, and I've never forgotten it. Even now, when walking some of Boston's meaner streets, I find myself moving like a knife, carving my way around people, cutting myself out of their picture and leaving nothing of myself behind but a hole.

Like most kids, I was aware that the world was filled with dangerous people, yet I wasn't certain I could always spot them coming. My dad, however, was a deadeye when it came to spotting the outlaw class. He had never been in prison, but he always seemed to know who had spent time in the "big house" or who was headed down that path.

In his own way he tried to warn me about going in their direction. When I was young, he would drive the family from Florida back to our hometown in western Pennsylvania to visit relatives. Once there, he'd troll the streets with me in our big Buick and point to guys he knew and tell me something wicked, or weird, or secret about them. "He killed a man with a pitchfork," Dad would say, nodding slyly toward some hulking farmer in bib overalls. "Look at his hands. He's a strong SOB—could strangle the life out of a cow."

Or Dad would point to a woman. "She had a kid when she was in ninth grade and sold it to a neighbor." He knew it all. "He burned down a barn. He shot a cop. He robbed a bank." Dad went on and on. I was always surprised at how many people from such a small town had been in prison. And I was really surprised that after committing such despicable acts they were back out on the street. They were a scary-looking lot, misshapen, studded with warts and moles, and I was glad we were in the car. But not for long. He'd take me to the Elks Club, or the Am-Vets hall, or Hecla Gun Club in order to get up close and personal with some of the criminal class. He'd order a beer and get me a Coke and some sort of food treat that came out of a gallon pickle jar of beet-red vinegar—a hard-boiled egg, or a swatch of pig's skin, or a hunk of kielbasa. Everything smelled like a biology specimen, and with the first bite the red juice spurted out and ran down my chin. I must have looked like I'd split my lip in a bar brawl. Then, once we were settled, Dad would continue to point out the criminals, all the while using his Irish whisper, which could be heard in the next town over. He pointed out bank robbers, church robbers, car thieves, and a shadowy "second floor" man, known for snatching jewelry from the bedrooms of sleeping home-owners. I began to imagine the entire town was some sort of bizarre experimental prison camp without walls—a punishment center where criminals were sentenced to living only with other criminals.

Dad snapped his fingers. "These folks zigged when the rest of the world zagged. And once you cross that line, there's no coming back. Mark my words."

All this was my father's way of letting me know he was in the know—he had the dirt on everyone, and it was the dirt that made them interesting. At the same time he made it clear they were damaged goods and could never come clean again. Dad's keen eye for spotting criminals of all stripes was impressive. But it wasn't perfect. He never had me pegged for being one of them.

Ironically, in spite of all the fear and remorse and self-loathing, being locked up in prison is where I fully realized I had to change my life for the better, and in one significant way I did. It is where I went from thinking about becoming a writer, to writing. I began to write stories—secret stories about myself and the restless men around me. While among them, I may have feigned disinterest, but like my father I watched them closely and listened whenever they spoke. Then back in my cell I would sit on the edge of my bunk with my journal spread open across my knees and try to capture their stories with my own words. For some paranoid reason the warden would not allow us to keep journals. He probably didn't want the level of violence and sex among both prisoners and guards to be documented. My secret journal was an old hardback copy of *The Brothers Karamazov* by Dostoyevsky, in which I spent hours writing in a tiny script between the tightly printed lines. I kept the book like a Gideons' Bible on top of my locker and, as far as I know, its true purpose was never discovered.

Someone once said anyone can be great under rosy circumstances, but the true test of character is measured by how well a person makes decisions during difficult times. I certainly believe this to be true. I made a lot of mistakes, and went to jail, but I wasn't on the road to ruin like everybody said. While I was locked up, I pulled myself together and made some good decisions.

Like any book about mistakes and redemption (Oscar Wilde's *De Profundis* is my favorite), the mistakes are far more interesting to read about (and write about)—so I'll start with where I think I went around the bend.

2 / misfit

I was nineteen, still stuck in high school, and I wasn't living at home. I had *unlimited* freedom. No supervision whatsoever. I had spending money. I had a fast car. I had a fake ID. My entire year was a grand balancing act between doing what I wanted and doing what I should, and being who I was while inventing who I wanted to be: a writer with something important to say.

During my junior year my parents had moved the family from Fort Lauderdale, Florida, to San Juan, Puerto Rico. My dad, who had a lifelong habit of switching jobs almost every year, took a position as a construction superintendent rebuilding a beachfront hotel and casino. My mom and my older sister were all for it; my younger brothers were ready to live like surfer boys. It sounded like a big party to me. I turned in my books, packed my bags, and said farewell to my few friends and teachers at Sunrise High School without shedding a tear. Since I had already gone to nine different schools, I was skilled at being a professional acquaintance. I didn't have a problem with saying good-bye to old friends and walking away forever. On the plane down to Puerto Rico I figured I'd never see them again, and I'm sure they thought the same of me. New friends were always around the corner.

I didn't speak Spanish so I couldn't go to the public schools in San Juan, and since my parents didn't have the money for private school we decided it would be best for me to just go to work. My dad fixed me up with the electrical subcontractor on his construction project, and right away I found myself wiring hotel rooms. The money was good. Half of the existing hotel was shut down while we added two new floors. A lot of the workers were from the States and one of the perks of the job was that they were given hotel rooms to live in. I was, too. This was ideal. I had privacy. I had my own TV. I even had maid service—didn't have to make a bed or pick a wet towel off the floor for half a year. Plus, my parents lived in an apartment a block away. Each evening after I showered in my hotel room, I would carry my dirty laundry down the street where I joined the family for dinner. Afterward, I'd go back to the hotel with clean laundry and play cards with the other electrical workers who lived down the hall. They were nice older guys who flew in from Miami every week to make fast money working double shifts. They let me drink a little, but not too much. And they let me lose a little, but not too much. On the weekends they'd fly home and I'd drink a little too much and wander around the tourist zones.

I'd go to the casinos at the El San Juan and Americana. I'd imagine I was James Bond meeting beautiful older women at the roulette tables and walking arm in arm up to their rooms where something dangerously exotic might happen. But the only arm I managed to warm up was on the slot machines. I loved playing them. The flashing lights and the sound of the gears spinning and the wild thrill of the jingling coins pouring into the metal pay-tray and the waitresses dressed in skimpy outfits bringing me free drinks for good tips was a blast. And if I lost too much I'd hop up and walk for an hour down the beach and look out at the stars and listen to the surf and inhale the whole world's briny smell rising from the ocean I loved. Then it never felt as if I had lost. And once, I had won so much I stood on the beach in the moonlight skipping silver quarters across the calm water as the little waves pawed the shore.

But after a while, I began to think of school again. Besides, I knew nothing about electricity and nearly electrocuted myself several times. After I had melted my third pair of Klein sidecutters and scorched a number of body parts while working on live wires, I admitted that electrical work was not in my future and I made the decision to get my high school diploma. After six months on the job I had saved enough money to afford a private school. But I couldn't get in. My grades had always been mediocre, and given that I had never finished eleventh grade, the private schools in San Juan wouldn't accept me as a senior. The thought of repeating eleventh grade was too depressing. I talked to my parents and they arranged for me to return to my cast-off school back in Florida and live with a family who had an extra room. My parents thought this was the best opportunity for me. I had my savings and had never been much trouble, so they must have reasoned it was an opportunity for me to spread my wings and make something of myself. I packed my bags, said good-bye to my family, and returned to Fort Lauderdale. When I reenrolled as a senior at Sunrise High, no one asked about the second half of my junior year, and I didn't volunteer any information.

It turned out that the people my dad arranged for me to live with—the Bacon family—were desperate for extra cash. My dad had met Fred Bacon while at an Elks Club benefit to help needy kids. The Bacons had purchased a new house with a swimming pool, had two new cars, and were raising two preschool kids, all on an income selling mail-order prosthetic limbs out of their garage—which looked like a morgue of plastic parts. Mr. and Mrs. Bacon had limb disabilities themselves—he with a missing arm and she without a left foot—and so were well suited for their business.

"Can't make a dime," Mr. Bacon said one night after a few

beers. He yanked off his flexible rubber arm and waved it overhead like a giant bug antenna. "All these old people come down here with prosthetics that look like something whittled out of a baseball bat. You'd think they would want something snazzy-looking. But no. They're just happy to be alive. In the meantime, we're starving."

So my rental money was welcome. Plus, with my new grocery store job at Winn-Dixie I was always bringing home bags full of dented cans, crushed boxes of cereal, half-open packages of dried beans and rice, and frozen food with freezer burn. The Bacon family didn't mind the misfit food, but soon they found out I was the greater misfit. It took them about six weeks to realize I was a live-in party crasher. After having my own hotel room in San Juan, I wasn't ready to live with other people. I'd go out drinking with my friend Will Doyle, and afterward I'd come home late and play my stereo at full volume, smell up the house with cigarette smoke, and make long-distance phone calls on the Bacons' bill. I kept drinking more and more until I discovered I could drink lots of beer. Nearly a case of it in a sitting. Unfortunately I was also in the process of discovering I had no tolerance for that much alcohol and I always became blind drunk and ferociously ill, spending almost every night loudly heaving my guts out in the toilet while begging God for mercy. I was a mess.

After one especially robust night of drinking with Will, I

stumbled home, crawled up the sidewalk, stabbed my key in the front door, let myself in, and power barfed all over the living room. After I sloshed blindly through that mess on all fours, I splattered the bathroom, my bedroom, the bathroom again, my bedroom again, until I passed out in the bathroom with my arms draped around the toilet and my head on the cool rim of the bowl.

When I came to the next afternoon, after the carpet cleaners had finished their work, I was summoned into the kitchen, which had been closed off with plastic sheeting and heavily sprayed with institutional-strength air freshener. I was promptly informed that I had to pack my bags and be out of their lives in an hour. Mr. Bacon tapped on the face of his watch—with his flexible prosthetic finger—to show that he meant *business*. I didn't debate their judgment of me as "an immature, spoiled brat who needed a major butt-kicking in order to straighten up." I didn't have time to defend myself. I suddenly felt sick all over again.

"Excuse me," I belched, and quickly covered my mouth with both hands, nodded my agreement to their assessment of my character, and ran down the hall to the bathroom.

Mrs. Bacon limped behind me yelling, "Don't you dare soil my carpet again!"

I didn't. But I threw up something so harshly acidic it left me with canker sores on the inside of my mouth.

As I stumbled out of the house, Mr. Bacon hollered out one final warning: "Keep this up and you'll fall flat on your ass."

I spit up on the grass.

I spent the night in my car, parked next to the Dumpster behind the grocery store. For a short while I felt sorry for myself, and then figured my drinking was a sign that I was living in the wrong place, with the wrong sort of people. There was no promise of anything in the Bacon family. The wife kept the kids in front of the TV all day while she vacantly dozed across the couch. If they acted up she'd swing at them with her cane. The husband was constantly worried about money and kept reminding me not to use too much electricity. He was so cheap he turned the hot water heater down to tepid. Even I knew enough to understand what Buddha meant when he said, "Always walk the road of happiness to prosperity." They seemed miserable and loveless. Nothing gave them pleasure because they were unable to receive it. And there I was, full of promise and hope and desire for real love and real events to shape and change my life. I knew I was free to change myself—free to feel the entire impact of what I was doing. And I wanted to feel it *all*. Being in that house was spoiling the hope of what life should offer. They were *trapped* and tapped out of ideas and cash and just waiting to collapse, and I was glad I wouldn't be around to watch it all happen.

Still I knew something had to be wrong with me, too. You just didn't end up homeless, hung over, sleeping in your car with all your worldly possessions because you had control of your life. I had lost control. Temporarily. But I'd get it back, I figured. I always did. My family had highs and lows, made money and lost what money can buy, had good days and days that were ground out like cigarette butts. So I was used to hitting the bottom. Now I was waiting for the bounce. By the time I fell asleep across my suitcases, I only felt sorry for the Bacon kids.

In the morning I woke up feeling pasty. My skin was like marzipan. I had slept with the windows rolled up and all that drinking had run me down. I bought a newspaper and coffee and looked through the Rooms to Rent section. I spotted a promising ad and drove over to an address on North Broward Boulevard. It was an old motel whose sun-faded sign barely read THE KING'S COURT. The sign was rimmed with broken bulbs that looked like rotten teeth.

I rang the office buzzer, and an old woman with brown wrinkled skin like a well-used pirate map opened the door and flicked a cigarette butt over my head. "Does the name Davy Crockett mean anything to you?" she asked.

"Yeah, he was king of the wild frontier," I said, quoting the theme song from the TV show.

"Well he was the *king* of the frontier," she said, then, pointing at her chest, added, "and I'm the *queen* of King's Court. I'm Davy Crockett the fourth, his great-great-granddaughter."

"Great," I said, thinking she looked old enough to be his daughter, but I liked her right off because she was the opposite of what I had just left.

"Now, what can I do for you?" she asked.

"I need a room," I said.

"Cash or welfare check?"

"Cash," I replied.

"Good, pay in advance and you'll get a ten percent discount."

I paid, and Davy's kin gave me the key to room number three. "It's a lucky room," she informed me. "To my knowledge, no one has died in it."

"I'll try to keep it that way," I replied, and turned to go.

"One more thing," she growled. "Don't make any trouble or I'll have to kick your tail out of here with Davy's moccasins."

I stared at her feet. Her beaded buckskins looked real to me.

"And I got his gun," she informed me. "Ole Betsy."

"Not to worry," I said, smiling. "Honest. I'm a good kid."

I moved my car around to the parking space with the big 3 painted on it. I unlocked the shiny brown door and in a glance saw it all—a ragtag furnished room with a tiny bathroom and shallow closet. A low-slung unmade bed took the middle of the room. Musty-smelling sheets were folded over an exhausted pillow. It was hot, there was no air-conditioning. Against a filthy wall was a dresser with a cheap lamp on it, and a cheaper fan. I turned the fan on and unpacked my belongings. I hung my shirts and pants on hangers. I placed my toiletries on a glass shelf above the sink. I pushed back the yellow shower curtain. The stale air trapped there smelled like a mildewed lemon. I put my shampoo on the edge of the tub. The wall tiles were yellow. The floors were yellow. I looked in the mirror. I was yellow. It was a color that did not look good on me.

I went back to the main room, pulled a chair over to the side of the bed, and stacked all my books on it. Then I sat down on the other chair. I suddenly felt drained, utterly exhausted, and held my head in my hands. My spirit was as beat as my body was tired. I had been reading Frank Conroy's *Stop-Time*. He had written about growing up in Florida. There was a passage about him dozing off and on all day in a backyard doghouse, like a panting animal in the heat. He was hiding from everyone, especially himself. I recognized the feeling. As much as I disliked the Bacons, I couldn't blame them for everything.

There was absolutely nothing I could think to do that

was good for me at that moment. I didn't have any plans. No big ideas. No hopes. No dreams. I was beat, inside and outside. I couldn't even make the bed or take a shower. Instead, I reached into my book bag, removed a pack of cigarettes, lit one, and exhaled. The fan bullied the smoke out the side window. I tried to fool myself into thinking that smoking was actually doing something, as if the smoke rising from my mouth was evidence of a churning industry that thrived inside me. But smoking wasn't doing any more than providing a physical activity that masked the emptiness behind it. I could blame the hollow feeling inside me on the hangover. But when the hangover passed, I knew I'd still sense that same barren internal landscape.

I needed to settle down and build a life for myself. For all I could tell, the King's Court was going to be where I planted my flag. Well, I thought, trying to lift my spirits, I'm not off to a good start but I should be merciful enough to give myself a second chance. After all, I figured I'd soon be saying the same thing to my parents.

I looked at my watch. It was time to get ready for work. Thank God for work, I thought. As I stood and headed for the shower, I felt a little bounce in my step. "I think I'm on an upswing," I said out loud. And I was.

3 / king's court

After my binge with the Bacons I settled down. I was drink-
ing less and reading more—and writing more, too, but with little luck. I needed help. I could write stuff down all day, but I
could never seem to organize it into anything worth reading.
My high school offered a creative writing course, but in order
to get in you had to have straight A's in eleventh-grade
English. I guess you had to show you were smart before being
allowed to take an "arty" course. I was still concerned the
principal would figure out I had never finished eleventh grade,
so I didn't put up a fight. I was glad I didn't when I found out
more about how the course was run. A friend who was in the
class said the teacher was just a wild-haired disorganized person masquerading as a wild-haired creative person. Every day
the teacher arrived and told her students to put a blank piece
of paper on their desks. Then she reached into her large carry-
all purse, fumbled around and pulled out some odd object,
steadied it on the wooden podium, and instructed the students

to "describe the object and remember to write with *flair*." So far they had described an artichoke, a butterfly press, a sneaker, a ring of keys, a potted hibiscus, a carved Christmas angel, and a sandwich. When I heard this, I knew I was doing better writing by myself no matter how skeptical I was of the results.

So I tried to be organized on my own. Ever since I'd been in elementary school I had kept diaries—but they were filled with the odds and ends of writing like a box full of jigsaw puzzle pieces, and there was no telling if they'd ever fit together. This time I arranged my journal in a series of sections. The first and most obvious was my daily entry section, which I filled with a wild stream of thoughts in a conscious effort to capture my honest feelings, true motivations, and crazed activities of each day. The writing was kind of a blinding kaleidoscopic view of my life.

The next section was my favorite. Each time I read a book, I cataloged the parts that struck me dumb with envy and admiration for their beauty and power and truth. I spent hours copying entire pages, word for word, in my small, cramped handwriting. After I read Richard Yates's novel *Revolutionary Road*, I copied out this passage:

> I still had this idea that there was a whole world of marvelous golden people somewhere. People who made their lives work out the way they wanted with-

out even trying, who never had to make the best of a bad job because it never occurred to them to do anything less than perfectly the first time.

The third section was plain and simple vocabulary building, where I'd write words and definitions I wanted to learn and use. Words like: viscous, impunity, paroxysm, unctuous, nefarious, onanistic, perfidious, lugubrious.

The fourth section was devoted to the moments of inspiration when book ideas came to me in full-color flashes, like bits of a film remembered, or a forgotten conversation suddenly pulsing to life. These were the great notions of sprawling novels that jolted me awake in the middle of the night or sneaked up on me as I drove my car so that I'd scrawl them on the white vinyl of the front seat next to my leg. Day and night I wrote down these ideas in my frantic, spastic penmanship. But that is all they ever amounted to—ideas. After recording them in my journal I'd flip through these pages, reading them to myself, pondering each idea, and rejecting them. All of them. But they weren't all lousy. I just didn't have the confidence and determination to sit still and nurture them properly. I couldn't seem to concentrate long enough to weigh the worth of each thought, isolate its potential, allow it to grow. Instead, my mistakes, self-doubt, insecurity, and wandering mind left me high and dry. It was never too long before I lowered my pen and set down my journal. It's the life of the mind that matters, I told myself as I picked up *The Catcher in the Rye* off my bedside stack. I figured my body would catch up later and write it all down. Of course, the body never did.

I decided my biggest writing problem was that I didn't have anything worthwhile to write about. Nothing interesting happened to me. Sure, living in a welfare motel for my senior year in high school was unusual, but it was not *extraordinary*. Or so I thought. But I had to keep practicing, and when the day came when something interesting did happen to me, I'd be ready. That's the best I could do, so I did it.

My school building had been a former prison. The city built a new prison, moved the inmates into their new quarters, then rehabbed the old prison and turned it into a high school. Members of the school board said the city was growing so fast they had no choice but to take advantage of existing structures. They removed the razor wire but kept the twelve-foot fence. The concrete guard towers were turned into headquarters for service clubs like Interact and Junior Achievement. There was a gate out front where the buses pulled up, and the principal could throw a switch in his office and the gate would automatically open and close. He seemed to enjoy that, and at the end of each day would announce on the intercom that we were "free to go." And we fled. The school cleared out in minutes, just as any prison would have if the warden opened the gate.

At Sunrise there were no prisoners left behind, but evidence of their trapped lives was everywhere. Even though the bars were removed I could still see the jagged edges above and below the windows where they had been unevenly cut with an acetylene torch. And in the right light no amount of fresh paint covered up what had been gouged into the concrete-block walls. Curse words, lovers' names, crude drawings of sex organs, sex objects, and sex acts. One wall was entirely worked into a life-size portrait of a naked woman reclining. I'd sit in a desk next to her and slowly trace the curves with my fingertips. It was sexy to imagine myself in prison. I'd let my mind drift and soon it was me behind bars as the snotty kid in *Jail Bait* saying, "I never thought that carrying a gun would lead to this!" I used to love watching those sleazy crime dramas on Saturday afternoon TV. My favorite was *The Violent Years*, about a gang of teenage girls dressed in black leather who robbed and molested guys like me. One of the girls said, "I shot a cop . . . so what!" I never knew girls like that and wondered what they might do to me if I was lucky enough to be captured by them.

I thought having my own place would automatically attract girls to me. I was mistaken. I was the spider who could not coax any flies into his web. I wanted girls to find me interesting. But maybe it was my whiny Holden Caulfield imitation of a boy in need of carnal therapy that got me nowhere. Or perhaps my sitting in the library with an intensely cheerless, poetic look on my face only scared girls away.

My big romance of the year was a crush on my psychology teacher, Miss Hall. It was her first year of teaching. She was fresh out of Ohio State. I'd sit in front of her desk and make troubled-brow faces which I thought illustrated the deep level of neurosis I represented. I figured she was watching me as closely as if I were a patient. It was only a matter of time, I figured, before she'd want to cure me, and I liked the idea that using a couch was part of the cure. I made straight A's for the first twelve weeks. Finally I got up the nerve to write her a letter about becoming a psychology and literature major. I didn't dare attempt a love letter—besides, I didn't have to. Any psychology teacher would know that a soul-baring letter from her most devoted student had hidden meaning.

After she received it she caught me in the hallway and whispered, "I need to speak with you tomorrow in my office." I could only imagine why she wanted me all alone. I figured I might start out talking about some personal observations inspired by Kesey's *One Flew over the Cuckoo's Nest*, then move on to a sensitive appreciation of Plath's *The Bell Jar* and its story of a woman's journey into madness. Then we could get more comfortable discussing *Love Story*.

But our talk had no room for literary seduction. She had already been seduced.

"I'm quitting," she revealed in confidence. "I'm pregnant. I just wanted you to know that I've enjoyed your attention this semester and hope you keep up the good work."

That ended that. She was gone in a week. We had substitutes for the rest of the year. We read the textbook chapter by chapter and took moronic mimeographed tests. My grades dropped to barely passing. I was bored.

I only saw Miss Hall once more. It was unfortunate timing, as I was in a spot of trouble. A kid from school, Tony Gorda, had sold me a new car stereo. It was still in the package. I paid him and then found out it wouldn't work with my car. He told me to return it to the store for another model. When I did, the sales person called security on me and two big guys swooped down and grabbed my arms. It turned out Tony had shoplifted the stereo. The two big guys hoisted me up and carried me across the parking lot toward my car. They wanted to check my trunk and see if I had any more "loot." As they carried me with my toes just barely ticking the asphalt, Miss Hall pulled up in her car.

"Is anything wrong, Jack?" she asked, eyeballing the two gorillas on either side of me.

"No, ma'am," I replied, trying to act casual as I smiled down at her, and her extended belly.

"Then have a good day," she said, and drove away.

For a psychology teacher, she didn't have much of an eye for spotting trouble when it poked her in the nose. No wonder she was in a family way.

After the gorillas found no loot in my trunk, they dragged me back into their cramped security office, where I signed a release allowing the store to keep the stereo. Then I was free to go—which I did, very quickly.

One afternoon the principal called the entire school down to the auditorium to meet some "special alumni." A traveling foursome of lifers from Raford State Prison had come to address us regarding the perils of criminal behavior. Earlier in their prison lives they had spent some time incarcerated where we were now going to school.

We filed down the dark halls and entered the former prison cafeteria. Once we took our seats the convicts parted the red velvet stage curtain and sat down on folding chairs. They wore broad-striped black-and-white uniforms and looked like they might launch into a rendition of "Jailhouse Rock" until a club-wielding guard joined them and announced, "These men you see here will never be released from prison. They regret their crimes, but it is too late for regret. Their lives are ruined, but they have volunteered to speak with you all today about the perils of a criminal life. Please listen carefully. Someday you will graduate, but you will not want to go to your class reunion dressed like these guys."

What could they say that would possibly change my life? I was enjoying my life just fine. I wasn't going to become a criminal. I was going to be a writer. And if not a writer, I wasn't sure what I might do, but I certainly had no interest in becoming a criminal.

The first prisoner stood up and strutted back and forth like a bowlegged bulldog. "I," he said dramatically as he punched himself hard in the chest, "have an anger problem." He told how bullies beat him up every day. He used to like reading, but the bullies ripped his books to shreds. At that moment he picked up a Yellow Pages from the stage and, to illustrate what the bullies did to him *and* his anger problem, ripped the book clean in half, tossing the two pieces over his shoulders. Kids laughed out loud. We couldn't help ourselves. The show seemed so ridiculously fake.

We kept laughing until the principal snapped his fingers at us. The prisoner went on to declare that he stopped reading and started fighting back, and kept on fighting back until he killed a man with his bare hands. Suddenly he thrust his fists toward us, and when he opened his hands they were glistening with stage blood. He was now serving a life sentence, and advised us to control our temper.

The next guy was little and nervous as a dragonfly. He

wore big round glasses and buzzed on about drugs in a whiny insect voice. First he'd smoked marijuana, then he took pills, then he started "mainlining heroin—China white—Iranian tar—Mexican brown." He went on to impress us with his knowledge of the opium-growing regions of the world. The more he talked about how good it had made him feel—"with the skinny needle in my arm and the blood blooming in the syringe"—the higher his voice rose. By the time he started using words like "rapture" and "sexiness," he was swooping around as if he were having a seizure. Finally, the guard cut him off.

"What he means to tell you," the guard summarized in case we missed the message, "is that once you start with drugs, you end up like him—a dope fiend who can only spend the rest of his days behind bars, dreaming of the past." He escorted the dragonfly back to his seat. I watched as he slumped forward in a memory high.

The third guy had been a mail thief as a kid. "I started out small," he announced. He went on to tell us about how he stole cash from birthday cards. Then checks. Then he robbed a string of banks and by misfortune he happened to shoot a bank guard and now was doing life. He advised us to work honestly for our money, and live within our means. Nobody seemed impressed with his reasonable advice, given where he was now spending all his time.

The last man was in for sex crimes. As he spoke, he never

raised his eyes above his shoes. When he was a boy he didn't have any friends to play with. He spent a lot of time alone. He didn't have much to do. He discovered masturbation. He wished he had exercised self-control and gone into the seminary. He never meant to hurt those women. In prison he said he had embraced the teachings of Jesus Christ and was a better man for it. He wanted us to forgive him. A halfhearted murmur of forgiveness broke out in pockets. I wasn't buying it. It seemed to me that no amount of forgiveness would ever wash away his need to be forgiven every day. He reminded me of the Flannery O'Connor story I loved, "A Good Man Is Hard to Find," where the Misfit shoots the hugely annoying grandmother to death and then says she would of been a good woman, if somebody had been there to shoot her every minute of her life.

Wouldn't we all.

As I watched the prisoners being marched away I knew there was nothing we had in common. I wasn't angry. I didn't use drugs. I didn't steal. I wasn't a rapist. But something was wrong. I felt adrift inside, as if I had a compulsion not to be myself. I especially had that feeling when I read books. I seemed to become the main character, as if I had abandoned myself and allowed some other person to step right in and take me over. It was a great ride becoming a fictional character for a day or a week, but when the temporary visitor left I felt as empty as a bottle, and when I regained my own voice it was always strangely scarred from the experience, as though something in me had been torn open and then healed over. But that didn't mean I'd end up in prison.

My friend Glen Martin's dad was a sales rep for Van Heusen shirts. He sold them to stores throughout south Florida. His garage was filled with shelves stacked with samples, and after each new season Glen's dad let him sell the samples to his friends. I was a good customer.

One afternoon I was in his garage sorting through new styles when he asked, "You ever smoke weed?"

"Ahh, no," I replied, sounding very uncool to myself.

"Want to try some?" he asked.

"Not now," I said. "I have to go to work."

"Tonight?" he asked. "Come over to my new friend James's apartment in the Lauderhill Lakes complex. Apartment 311. We're having a weed party there."

"Okay," I said. "Yeah." I was trying to sound enthusiastic, but it wasn't working. I bought a shirt and left.

All through my shift at the grocery store I was absent-minded. I had read lots of books where people smoked weed. Some seemed to really enjoy it and got happy and hungry and silly and had deep insights into themselves and the world. I had a sneaky suspicion I was going to be the other kind of smoker—the kind I had also read about who go off the deep end and let life drift way out of control, and become dependent on dope and other users to help them out, and are abused and broken down and the only deep insight they gain from the experience is that they have totally ruined their lives—and I'd end up like that girl from *Go Ask Alice* who went nuts on LSD and was locked in a closet after she imagined a million bugs were on her skin and to kill them she clawed off all her flesh and nearly bled to death.

By the time I finished restocking the entire canned vegetable section at work I was convinced I would be a vegetable if I smoked. Yet I went to the apartment. Why? For the same deadhead reason people climb mountains—it was there and I wanted to try it. Plus, there was the slim possibility it would make me a better writer. I got that impression from reading William Burroughs.

I knocked on the door. James answered. He was at least ten years older than the rest of us.

"Come in," he whispered, and as I entered the room I turned and saw him peek out the doorway as if I might have been followed by the police. He was so paranoid he scared me.

Inside, the apartment was filled with smoke that smelled like an acrid palmetto brushfire. I coughed. On the living room floor Glen and four other guys were sitting cross-legged around a tall brass-and-glass hookah. Jefferson Airplane was on the stereo. Glen grinned up at me.

"We're trying to get high but it's not working," he said, disappointed. "We're just down to stems and seeds. Want a toke?"

He gave me the spitty plastic end of the hookah hose. I drew in some smoke and instantly hacked it out of my lungs.

"I know what you mean," he remarked. "We even filled the hookah with wine but it can't take the burn out of this stuff."

I nodded my head in agreement as I gritted my teeth from trying to suppress more coughing. After it was determined the stems and seeds were a bust, I spent the rest of my time wondering just how long I had to hang around before politely leaving. I drank two beers, then said so long to Glen and James and the other guys I never met. They had stared at the floor the entire evening as if it were interesting. It just looked filthy to me.

All the way to my car I expected cops to grab me by the shoulder just as they had when I was exchanging the hot stereo. I didn't want to be busted and thrown in jail so that someday I could tell my sad tale to others, just as the prisoners had told their woeful tales to me.

When I made it home I closed and double locked my door and pulled the curtains.

"I don't have to do that again," I said to myself. But I must not have been listening.

I lived in the King's Court for the whole school year. Davy baked and left cookies on my bed, and she always monitored my health and mothered me with homemade soup when I was sick. Her motel catered to a patchwork of local folks who were down on their luck. Florida was still pretty segregated, so the cultural mix was unique and mostly peaceful—blacks, whites, Hispanics, and some Seminoles. Every now and again the Seminoles would get drunk and claim that Florida was their territory and everyone else had better pack up and move out. Parents made sure the kids were inside and the doors locked during these tirades. Davy let them shout and parade around in their native costume as they called on the spirit of Chief Osceola to help them regain their homeland. She only pulled out Ole Betsy and called them a bunch of "alligator wrestlers" when they walked onto Broward Boulevard to scare cars, or when they busted up furniture and threw bottles of Ripple and Boone's Farm through the jalousie windows. She never called the cops on anyone. Her frontier policy was to work it out among ourselves. Besides, she felt for the Seminoles.

"They got every right to be pissed," she said. "It wasn't so long ago the government paid two hundred dollars bounty for every Indian killed by settlers."

When I told my school friends where I lived they thought I was joking. For most of them I might as well have been living in the Black Hole of Calcutta. When my drinking buddy, Will, came to visit, he was always nervous his new Camaro would get broken into or stolen. And when any of the motel kids knocked on my door for a treat (I always kept bags of candy from the store in my room), my friends reeled back in horror as if the kids had lice, ringworm, or rabies. But after meeting my neighbors they'd relax and realize that people on the other side of the tracks were warm-blooded, could tell good stories, and were as curious about white high school kids as we were about them. I named my room the "Bad Attitude Clearing House."

Things were not going well for my dad's business. The family had moved from Puerto Rico to St. Croix in the Virgin Islands with the hope that my dad could start a small construction company and make big money. He started the company, but there was not much money and my mom was worried. I had stopped asking for a monthly allowance. I just wanted to be one less thing to fret about. That was my goal. My letters home were lame, but they did not add to the general gloom and doom around the house. Even when I changed my mind and decided not to go to college, it didn't bother them.

At first I was going to go. I had taken all the tests that counted—the SAT and the Florida Placement Exam in order to determine state college eligibility. There was only one kid out of our 700-student graduating class who was going to Harvard, and that was *not* me.

After I was accepted to the University of Florida in Gainesville, the only school I applied to, I was required to attend an interview with the admissions office. Before I went up to Gainesville I looked over the course offerings. The school was strong in literature but just seemed so-so in creative writing. That bothered me, but not too much because I was accustomed to not getting everything I wanted.

On a Wednesday I took off work time, packed a bag, and drove up the turnpike to I-75. I had changed the oil in my car, and had the brake pads replaced and the engine tuned. The car drove beautifully. I loved my car. I felt even more comfortable in it than I did in my room. They were about the same size and had about the same amount of furniture and closet space.

I arrived on campus early. I drove around the dorms, the library, the classroom buildings, and the administration offices. It was 1971 and the campus was dozing. Across the country students were rioting over civil rights, Vietnam, social justice, and government cover-ups involving tapping phones and secret wars. While in high school I accepted that I was living in a void, but now that I was heading for college I needed some fresh air and fresh thinking. Granted, my mind was pretty blank to begin with, and I wasn't exactly sure what I wanted or what I needed, but I was totally certain what I *didn't* want. And I didn't want the University of Florida. It looked just like a big, sprawling high school. It was everything I feared, and it gave me the creeps. As I drove around I came to the conclusion that I wasn't going to go. I wasn't going to just bump along to grade thirteen and not go to a real school where I'd be roughed up and challenged. By the time I parked my car and entered the admissions officer's cubby, I was determined. The lady who met with me was very nice. She shook my hand and welcomed me to the college. She gave me a little booster bag full of university items: a mini orange football with a Gator logo, a Gator car decal, a Gator hat, a Gator hand towel, a Gator mug, and a rubber Gator for the top of my car antenna.

I thanked her for the items and set them down by my feet. I was trying to come up with a way to tell her why I decided against attending the school. I suddenly wanted to blame it all on the Gator mascot, but knew I needed more than that, and more than just a gut feeling that the place was all wrong for me. Then she sealed the deal while pointing out a few freshman rules.

". . . and you have to dorm on campus for the first two years, and during that time you cannot have a car."

I stared at her. I debated silently if I should tell her I loved my car—needed my car—and that I had been living on my own long enough to *never* want a roommate. But I kept my thoughts to myself. I smiled. We chitchatted a bit and I left, and on the way home I felt a huge weight lift from my shoulders. All the way down to my toes I knew I had made the right decision. But I didn't know entirely why. I guessed I would find out later. It was a good guess.

4 / pair of jacks

Like every guy, I had read On the Road by Kerouac and wanted to cut loose and carom from coast to coast as he did without thinking of money or trouble or *anything* but the great freedom that awaited me like a ship heading to sea. I was looking for a change. I wanted to see something beyond high school and the King's Court and a grocery-store aisle lined with canned vegetables. And I was especially itchy to feel new things, to shed my skin and grow. I couldn't explain myself to anyone because I was only full of excited urges and notions and desires, kind of like the Hulk before he transforms. Plus, I had a strong sense that I needed to snap off my past in order to have a future. All year I had worked hard to keep myself together. I held my job, managed my own money, kept passing grades, and stayed out of deep trouble. But now my accomplishments just seemed like survival routines, and I wanted to move on to more romantic turf and find out who I was and what might happen to me when the rubber met the road. And, of course, I wanted to write. I figured if I crisscrossed Florida from coast to coast as if I were tying up the laces on a high-top sneaker I would eventually stumble on something *juicy* to write about. I was full of hope. I had been reading constantly. I kept up my daily journal-writing routine, logging my favorite quotes and building my vocabulary. And now it was time for me to stop being a chippy high-school writer and to challenge myself.

So I began to shut down the "Bad Attitude Clearing House." I gave away all my thrift-shop furnishings to whoever would take them. I gave my suit and jacket and striped shirts and club ties and wing tips to a young guy who was looking for work. I kept my T-shirts and jeans and sneakers. I rounded up the little kids and passed out all my candy stash, which they gleefully devoured. They didn't save one piece for later. And as I watched them prance and dance around the parking lot like sugared-up puppets, I told myself to stop rationing pleasure as if it were a paycheck. It was time to cut loose and have fun, and not worry about tomorrow. I wanted my candy, too.

Reading *On the Road*, I felt more like Sal Paradise than Dean Moriarty. Sal was in love with everything and everybody. His eyes were as wide open as his heart. He recorded what he saw and what he felt in equal amounts, as if he were balancing the great scales of observation and reflection. But Dean confused me. He just wanted to consume everything. He had to keep moving like a shark, and in the end he was a tragic ghost of a person instead of a stream of milky way jazz under open highways. I wanted to move like Dean, but I wanted Sal's heart and soul.

Unlike Sal and Dean, I didn't have years to string out a trip. I had just over two weeks for a mini–*On the Road* adventure. I knew I was going to join my family in St. Croix. But first, I figured I'd drive up to Jacksonville, see Stephen Crane's house, then work my way down the state to Key West and Hemingway's home, and finally drive back to Miami to ship the car. That was all the structure I wanted. As Kerouac wrote, "I was a young writer and I wanted to take off. Somewhere along the line I knew there'd be girls, visions, everything; somewhere along the line the pearl would be handed to me."

I wanted that pearl.

I had spoken with my dad and told him I was putting off college and instead would help with his new company. I wasn't any good at construction, but I could drive the truck to pick up the crews and deliver supplies and work odd tasks in between. I told him I'd be home in a few weeks. He said he was counting on me, and it felt good to be needed by him. We could spend some time together after such a long break, and I could save money for a college that was a better fit for me. I called a shipping company and made a date to ferry my car to

St. Croix out of Port Everglades. I booked an air ticket for my-self and thought that helping my father, saving a few bucks, and writing on my own was all the purpose I needed.

Then, out of the blue, something happened that I hadn't planned on. My friend Tim Scanlon called. He wanted to visit. He graduated a year ahead of me and had been going to Florida State to study medicine on a full scholarship. He was a smart guy and I knew him only because we had worked to-gether at the grocery store. I didn't know any of his other friends and he didn't know mine. The only reason he wanted to stay with me is he didn't want his parents to know he was in town. He wanted to have some fun before he settled in with them for the summer. I told him he could hide out at my place for a few days, but then I was leaving. That was good enough for him.

I picked Tim up at the train station. He had changed in the last year. His hair was down to his shoulders. He wore a pair of ripped-up jeans and a Hendrix T-shirt. He looked like he hadn't slept in a week, and by the time he got to my car he had already lit a joint.

"Want some?" he asked.

I hesitated and started the engine.

"I'm in pre-med," he said. "It can't hurt you."

I took a puff, then another. After a few minutes I fell silent and all my thoughts seemed big, very big, so endlessly BIG I couldn't get out of them. My brain hummed along as one thought segued into another. The concentration was incredible. If I had been reading a book, each page would have been the size of a Kansas wheat field. The space inside my mind seemed endless.

After a while he tapped me on the shoulder. "Good stuff," he remarked.

I forgot I was driving. "Did I run any lights?" I asked in a panic.

He grinned. "I don't know," he replied, and shrugged. "I wasn't paying attention."

I had already quit work, so we just lounged around my room for a few days. We were so high we hardly went out. The weed dazed us until we got hungry enough to drift down the street to a pizza parlor, where we'd order two for-one large specials and burn sheets of skin off our upper palates on the first bite. Then, with food in our bellies, we'd straighten up a bit and go back to the room and smoke a joint and settle down to talk up a storm. He liked my books.

"I guess you read a lot," he said, digging through the open boxes. "You ever read *Hallucinogens & Shamanism* by Harner?"

"Never heard of it," I replied.

"He's incredible," he said. "He believes that hallucinogens

are the way we get in touch with our animal past. That in our DNA is stored genetic memories of when we were an evolving species and when you take the stuff the Indians of Brazil take you'll access your genetic library all the way back to cellular experience."

That seemed impressive to me. He talked about a lot of books I'd never heard of. Scientific books on animal communication. Studies on dancing bees by Karl von Frisch. Reports on enzyme exchange communication between termites. And a book called *Insect Societies* by Edmund O. Wilson that linked human behavior to animals from apes to insects.

"All behavior is chemical," he said, getting so excited he stood up and paced the room and beat his fists against his thighs. I pegged him as my Dean Moriarty and was happy he showed up with his wild genetic ideas. "Your memory is just chemistry. Your motivations. Your *everything*. You have to read the stuff I read," he insisted. He wrote out a frenzied list, and with each title he let out a hiss of excitement, pushed the hair out of his eyes, and pronounced each book better than the last. "This stuff on bio-communication is the future," he said. "It will take you back to the *why* of everything. Remember when you were a little kid and kept asking *why* and your parents gave you some half-baked answers? Well, these books get down to the root of the *why*. If you understand this stuff you will understand everything—religion, politics, psychology, art—the history of all human desire is entirely in our *chemistry*."

He knew great stuff about biology and chemistry and medicine. I knew something about literature and what people plotted in their hearts and thought and suspected, but he knew the secret *why* behind each thought. I only knew how it looked once it happened, once it went *splat* in my face, and suddenly I wanted to know the *why* to everything. It seemed the most important desire I'd ever known.

"You have to read more science, man," he encouraged. "It's opening doors on behavior. I mean, literature is good. But the literature of the future is going to be based on genetics, not on environment. Believe me, the stuff we are learning is *heavy*."

Right away I was disappointed that I wasn't going to college. I had always believed in the maxim that the best way to predict the future was to create it. Now, the future appeared inaccessible to me. Without science I was just another stimulus-response cave dweller howling at the moon.

"I got lousy grades," I said, feeling as if I had already wasted my entire life.

"Don't sweat it," he sneered. "You could go to any college in the world. You've got more than grades, you've got brains."

"But no money," I concluded. "Which is actually worse than being an idiot."

"Well, I can help you there," he started. "Let's sell some

weed and make some cash." He ran his hands through his long blond hair. "We'll drive up to Tallahassee and cop from the guys in the lab there. They grow the most potent stuff—hydroponically. None of the throat-burning yard twigs you cop from hippies which makes you jumpy. The lab stuff is mind-blowing—better than Thai stick."

"Yeah," I said. I was totally caught up in his vision. He knew things I had never considered, had never heard of. He was on a roll, and I was ready to roll with him.

"Let's hit the road," I said.

It took me about a minute to load my car. I trotted over to Davy's place and turned in my key and gave her a big hug and a gift I'd been saving for just this moment.

She peeled off the wrapping paper. It was a signed photo of Fess Parker, who had played Davy Crockett on the TV show. I'd found it in a thrift store.

"I love it!" she hooted. "You always have a place here, so keep in touch."

As much as I loved Davy's, I left the King's Court feeling some vague relief that my high school year in a motel was over, but before I could consider what that relief meant I was swallowed up by the excitement of the adventure. I drove directly to the grocery store and cashed a check for three hundred dollars, which was half of my savings. I gave Tim two hundred for the score.

By the time we got up to Tallahassee it was dark. We checked in to a motel and he made a few calls.

"We're in luck," he said, setting down the receiver. "They've just dried a fresh crop and are plucking off the buds."

I drove him over to the school lab and dropped him off. He had a student ID and could hang out there until the dope was ready. I went back to the motel room to wait for his call.

Four hours later I was still waiting, and I began to think that something went wrong. Maybe he wasn't coming back. Maybe he'd been arrested. Maybe he'd ripped me off. I watched TV until I fell asleep. At sunrise I tried to drive onto the campus, but without a student ID I was stopped by security at the front gate. I returned to the motel and waited in my room until checkout time. Then I went down to the lobby and sat there all day trying to read the newspaper, but every time the phone rang, which was every few minutes, my head jerked toward the clerk, who was sympathetic enough to shake his head, no, no, no, with each call. At dusk I told myself I would leave at sundown. At sundown I told myself I'd give it just a little more time. I left at nine, when it was pitch-black out.

I did the best I could to rub him and the rip-off out of my mind by returning to my original plan. I got in my car and kicked my butt straight across the state to Jacksonville. In the morning I found where Stephen Crane had lived and sat in front of his house reading *The Red Badge of Courage*, which was so good I couldn't figure out why I hadn't read it earlier. Henry Fleming's convictions impressed me. His desire to fight. His fear of being a coward. His renewed battle courage. Suddenly I felt incredibly lucky. Like Henry, I sensed I was enlisting in something great, too—writing—and that it was time for me to stop running away from it, but to face it head on.

I was charged up with a renewed desire to write. I hopped in my car and blew out of Jacksonville and drove all day in the rain like a maniac toward the Keys. I stopped in Melbourne to get some gas and thought of Jim Morrison singing about how people are strange. I looked around the gas station—they sure were. I jumped back in my car and got going. Once I passed Miami I began to see a steady stream of cars coming the other way, and I noticed no one but me was heading for Key West. I fiddled with my radio until I found a report that an early tropical storm was shifting north from Cuba and might hit the keys with hurricane force winds by nightfall. I gunned my car and sped down the causeway, skipping from key to key until I arrived in Key West. It was already raining sideways and the palm trees were wagging their leaves at me. I laughed out loud. It was thrilling. The whole place was boarded shut and taped up, but nothing could stop me from being there in the middle of it. I was still pumped on Henry Fleming's courage. He was waving a flag and I was carrying a pen.

I found a motel made of cinder blocks and checked in. I got a good rate. Then I went down to a gas station store and bought what candles, water, and food were left. When I returned to my room I flicked the TV to the storm report and watched the almost-a-hurricane head our way. It never developed into more than a gale with eighty-mile-an-hour gusts. It passed over us in the night, dumping a foot of rain and blowing down the weak trees. The greatest damage was done to the tourist industry. The vacationers had fled. Of course, it didn't help that the TV stations played *Key Largo* on one channel and a documentary on the "Great Hurricane of 1935" on the other. That hurricane had killed over eight hundred people who were fleeing by rescue train when a twelve-foot surge of water, whipped up by two-hundred-mile-an-hour winds, swamped the passenger cars and took them all away. When the bodies were finally collected, they were burned in tall pyres like Hindus on the Ganges. And when the rescuers ran out of driftwood, they buried the rest in mass graves.

In the morning, when I emerged from my room, the locals were out and about cleaning up the mess, and a few drunken tourists were still celebrating their victory over nature. But the rest had fled and left the place to me. Right away I started making my rounds. First, I went to Ernest Hemingway's house. He had killed himself on my birthday. My tenth birthday. He took a shotgun, put the barrel in his mouth, and pulled the trigger with his toe. My dad had read *The Old Man and the Sea* to me because it was a fishing story.

"I'd have shot myself, too," he said after reading the obituary in the paper, "if it took me that long to catch a fish."

Hemingway's house had survived the storm, except that the giant swimming pool was filled with brackish water and debris, along with a magnificent sea turtle that I immediately named Ernest. I imagined the big man as wide across his back and tanned as the dark turtle and just as unflappable as it did a slow breaststroke from end to end.

I untangled an aluminum lawn chair which had blown into a manchineel tree. I sat down with my writing journal and grinned like an idiot. Just describing that huge, brooding turtle lumbering from end to end was inspiring. I was so happy to be the first one on the scene and wrote down all my impressions—just as Hemingway did in Spain during their civil war, and Crane after the sinking of the *Commodore*. Suddenly I remembered that John Hersey lived in Key West. His on-the-scene reportage of Hiroshima after the atomic bomb was incredible. These guys had gone into the heart of something raw and humanly transforming and had survived to write great books. They got their beginning as writers by going where the action was—to war—and I could, too. With Vietnam on fire the army was taking everyone they could get, but there was no guarantee I could be a journalist like Hersey. Instead, I could end up more like George Orwell and take a bullet through the neck. And there was something else—as much as I despised the war, deep inside I felt I was a coward. Like Henry Fleming I figured when the bullets started chewing up the ground around me I'd duck and run. I depressed myself. The only thing I had to write about was a turtle in Hemingway's pool. Moments before it seemed so romantic. Now it seemed mundane.

In order to buck up I went searching for John Hersey's house. Maybe seeing where he lived would give me another boost of courage. I got in my car and drove to a market. There were guidebooks to Key West but none of them gave his address. He was mentioned after Tennessee Williams and Elizabeth Bishop, whose addresses were listed. I went to the Williams house. It looked fine except the little white gazebo he built for Jane Bowles had toppled over. I had read *A Streetcar Named Desire* and *The Glass Menagerie* and, like everyone, I thought Williams was a genius. I hadn't read Jane Bowles's work but knew her husband's book *The Delicate Prey*, which was just about my favorite collection of stories in the world. Paul Bowles had gone to Morocco to write about Moroccans. I was hoping that St. Croix might be interesting to write about. Maybe I could begin to write something important there.

I drove down to Elizabeth Bishop's small house. I hadn't read her poetry and wished I had. Someone once said that all writers should read into their weaknesses. And I was weak in poetry. But nothing could blunt my happiness. Fate, it seemed, had brought me down to Key West. Fate brought the storm. And I felt fated to write. I still didn't have anything significant to write about so I just smoked another joint and recorded observations and reflections—just like Sal Paradise.

And like Sal, I missed my Dean Moriarty. I wondered what had happened to Tim Scanlon, so I called his home in Plantation, Florida. His mom answered.

"Is Tim there?" I asked.

"You aren't Jack, are you?" she asked harshly.

I told her I was Dave, "his other friend."

"Hey," he said when he came to the phone, "what's goin' down?"

"What happened, man?" I asked. "I waited forever at the motel."

There was silence. I thought I could hear his mother close a door. Finally he replied, "It was awesome. I had to sample the crop. It was like pure THC and sent me into a total genetic high. I couldn't tell where I was. Finally I walked around the campus in a trance until security picked me up and called my folks. They had to drive up and get me and now they're royally *pissed*."

"What happened to the weed?" I asked.

"Oh, well, the good news is the security people were pot-heads and they just kept the stash. But the bad news is we lost all your money."

I took a deep breath. Money wasn't easy for me to come by.

"I'll pay you back when I get working," he said. "Promise."

I didn't listen to much after that, and when I got off the phone I didn't know what to think.

I retreated to Sloppy Joe's bar, where Hemingway drank and played cards with his mob of friends who would then go out in his yacht and try to spot and sink Nazi U-boats with hand grenades. I sat at the bar and read *A Moveable Feast* and cried with a kind of jealous disappointment because that beautiful time in history had passed me by and the contrast between the lush enchantment of Europe and my welfare-motel life was suddenly very sad indeed.

But I dried my eyes and after a few beers and a couple of joints around back I imagined the great books I might write. Of course, I didn't write a word. It was easier to smoke joints and have someone deliver drinks than it was for me to deliver sentences.

The next morning I woke up with blisters on my forearms and hands. I was a born-and-bred Catholic and thought immediately it was some sort of writing stigmata and that I should get to a church. But then I remembered the chair at Hemingway's house had been lodged in a manchineel tree and must have been coated with a little bit of the tree's caustic sap. Ponce de León died from a manchineel-sap-coated arrow, and I figured I was a dead man, too. But after a few days of itching I figured it must have been the arrow that killed him, because I recovered just fine.

1 / st. croix

From the first week I landed in St. Croix I became part of a drug culture. Drugs were available everywhere at all times. Especially reefer. You could smell it on every other breath of air. In bars, on street corners, in passing cars, on buses, at the beach—people grew it in their home gardens and smoked it like cigarettes. It was so much a part of everyday life even the local police didn't bother with it, which is why the island was also a depot for smugglers. The U.S. customs office was kept busy inspecting oil tankers from the Middle East which supplied crude oil to the refinery at Hess Oil. That left sailboats and speedboats from the British and French and Dutch and independent islands to slip into St. Croix at night and unload their cargoes of marijuana and pharmaceuticals from Europe and underground labs. Then U.S.-registered pleasure boats would haul the cargo up to Florida, where it was easy to unload into trucks at any backyard dock along the intercoastal waterway.

But all I did was smoke it. I never thought dope would

lead to trouble, and I certainly had no idea it would land my ass in jail.

While I was in Key West smoking dope and wondering when I would find my writer's voice, everything in St. Croix had changed. Racial tension in St. Croix had always run high. There were a lot of white haves and a lot more black have-nots. The tension mounted when a radical black party, based on the Black Panthers, formed and publicly called for white extermination. The racial divide widened, and the anger boiled. Homes were broken into. People were murdered. Stores were looted. Hotels hired extra security to patrol the grounds and beaches. Tourism dropped.

The news media picked up the story and before long the wealthy white people who were living in the States and building retirement homes in St. Croix decided to cancel their house jobs. It was that sudden. Now, nobody was working, black or white.

The story must have been reported in the Florida papers, but in Key West I was "too busy" to read one and didn't hear about the situation until after I arrived. By then, it was too late to turn around. All my father's building jobs had been canceled. I was trapped. Instead of finding ourselves building new homes or hotels, my father and I worked at building large wooden packing containers to fill the need of the hundreds of people who were scrambling to empty their homes and ship their belongings off island. The white exodus was on.

All day I built crates. Because money was tight I didn't draw a paycheck and instead reluctantly agreed with Dad to be paid in room and board. With the little money I brought from the States I just managed to keep gas in my car. And there was no way I was going to save money for college. After my year of racial harmony at the King's Court I found the turmoil in St. Croix very disturbing. I understood the black point of view, but there was no way I could get them to see my sympathies. I was just another white target on legs. The level of anger was beyond reason. Black activists were preaching white extermination and the place was getting ready to explode. It wasn't long before I wondered if I could build a crate and ship myself off the island.

One morning after I had just smoked a joint rolled from old roaches a man came in with hand-drawn plans for a crate which included a false bottom about four inches deep. I remember him in detail. His name was Rik. He was in his late twenties, blond, shag haircut, green eyes, and a silver-dollar-sized circular burn scar on his forehead. When I asked about the scar he said it came from being shot with a flare gun.

"What was that like?" I asked.

"Blinding," he said dryly.

I didn't ask more, but he said he was shipping art and archaeological artifacts that needed extra protection. Fine, I thought, let him ship the crown jewels. It was none of my business.

After work I went down to the dockside bar where all the whites tanked up on duty-free Heineken.

I took a seat at the bar, next to my dad. As I looked across the room I spotted the guy with the scar sitting by himself. "What do you think of that guy?" I asked.

My dad took one look at him and had him pegged.

"He's a dope smuggler," he replied.

"How do you know that?" I asked.

"Just do," he said. "It's a gift I have."

I told him the guy had ordered a crate with a false bottom.

"He probably wants to smuggle cash or dope or gold into the States."

"Maybe," I said. "Or maybe he has Indian artifacts or pottery or stuff he doesn't want shippers to find."

"Don't be naïve," he said. "I've got his number. Dope is his game. But I don't give a damn where his money comes from as long as it helps get us off this rock."

I felt the same way. I wanted off.

Since I didn't have much money it didn't matter how lousy the bookstores were, and the library was little help. It was so hot and humid inside I had to scrape the mold off the spines of the books in order to read the titles. Nine out of ten books I looked up were missing. The librarians just shrugged when I mentioned the apparent theft problem. And if I complained too much they turned up their desk radios and played at being busy.

Because I couldn't find the books I wanted, I read what was available. The biographies were closest to the ocean and were especially moldy and not as desirable for the thieves. I read a few books about revolutionaries: Che Guevara, Emma Goldman, an odd book titled *Mutual Aid* by Peter Kropotkin, who was an anarchist, and a book by Alexander Berkman titled *ABC of Anarchism*. All this political reading made me think the island was ripe for an all-out race riot and political revolution just like the Haiti Graham Greene had written about in *The Comedians*.

Since I was trying so hard to make books lead my life, I didn't want to read them and then just put them back on the shelf and say, "good book," as if I was patting a good dog. I wanted books to change me, and I wanted to write books that would change others.

I was still trying to find something significant to write about and so, like all those political writers, I realized the only thing for me to do would be to jump right into the middle of the racial tension and use my wits. I remembered reading a quote from a newspaper journalist that stuck with me: "Where there is blood, there is ink."

I thought I'd put that quote to work. I got my notebook and a pen and ventured down to the Black Revolutionary Party headquarters to see if I could interview any of the leaders. There were about twenty black guys sitting under fluorescent lights in an old warehouse. They were playing cards and drinking rum. The walls were covered with Black Power posters, pictures of Malcolm X, and green, red, and black maps of Africa. When I walked in, all heads turned toward me. It wasn't quite like stepping into a military ambush, or being on the front lines in Spain, or witnessing the aftermath of an atomic bomb, but the atmosphere around me was definitely hostile.

There was a man in the back sitting at a desk. I assumed he was the leader. He had an Afro-pick stuck in his ball of black hair and he was talking loudly to someone on the telephone. When he saw me he abruptly hung up and gave me a long, studied look.

"What you want, white boy?"

That question sure cut to the chase and everyone watched to see how I'd take it.

There was no going back. "I'm looking to interview someone about the race relations," I replied. "They seem pretty bad to me, and I want to know more."

"What's there more to know than what you can see with your own eyes?" the man shot back. "The white people own the island and the black people work it like wage slaves."

That brought loud agreements from the other men, but they seemed to laugh and enjoy the situation more than be angry. For the moment, the oddness of my showing up was funnier than it was confrontational. That was a relief, but I wasn't sure how far I could keep going.

"I guess I want to know what you are going to do about it. I mean, how are you going to go about getting your share?"

"See," the man said, pointing at me, and looking to the other men in the room as if he were a preacher, "see, this question goes directly to the heart of the matter. Because we don't want a share of what we own, we want *all* of what we own. And that is the issue that cannot be solved with the white man unless we come to blows."

I stood still, and felt instantly trapped inside a stage play of rehearsed hostility. I looked from side to side as much as I dared. The anger was so sudden I was afraid to make eye contact with anyone for fear they might make something personal of it. And I couldn't tell if my courage had evaporated or if it was common sense that told me to get out of there, so I just asked, "Well, do you have a book I can read, or some material that will explain what your goals are? And then I can understand it all a bit more, and we can talk about it later?"

"What's to understand?" a man sitting to one side asked. "He already told you: the island belongs to the black man, so the black man is going to take what is his and be done with it. We don't need to make it more clear than that."

"Thank you," I said, and like some cub reporter I began to scribble a few words down on a small pad of paper. My hand was shaking badly.

"Besides," the first cut in, "how can we trust you?"

I didn't answer.

But another man did. "Give him a gun," he suggested. "Give him a gun and let him go out there and shoot a white man dead. Then we'll trust him."

I started to back away.

"Yeah. Give him a gun. If he's on our side, let him show it."

"I can't do that," I said.

"Then here's some advice," the same man continued, pointing a finger as black as the barrel of a gun at me. "Don't be coming in here as if you can play with the big boys. Revolution is serious business. You just turn your white ass around and go back to the white bar you come from and drink a cold white man's beer while you can because as the song say, 'When the revolution comes, Hertz is not going to put *you* in the driver's seat.' "

I knew it, too. "Okay," I said, turned around and fixed my eyes on the door, and as I walked toward it, I hoped I would make it. And when I did make it, I walked quickly to my car and took off with both hands on the wheel to keep them steady. I drove directly to the all-white bar and ordered a drink. I didn't know what to do next so I went out back and smoked a joint, then returned and ordered another drink. And another. I should have taken out my journal and written about what had happened. But I was so afraid of the incident I ran from it rather than write it down. Somehow, I didn't trust myself. I didn't trust that my own words would make a difference to anyone, black or white—even if the ink was blood red.

A few nights later Rik stopped by the warehouse. My dad was gone and I guess that was the moment he knew he could talk to me about his big plans. He wanted to pack the crate and have me screw it together, as he didn't have a screw gun. Before we got busy he pulled out a hash pipe and a piece of hash the size of a candy bar.

"You mind?" he asked.

"Fire it up," I said.

He cut off a gram and lit the pipe. He took a big hit and

passed it to me. We went on like this, loudly inhaling and exhaling, until the pipe was finished.

He went to his car and returned with a stack of square plastic containers about the size of cigar boxes. The edges were sealed with silver duct tape. We both knew they were filled with hash. What else could it be? But I didn't say anything. He slipped them into the false bottom, wedged them tightly together with wadded-up newspaper, then I screwed down the next layer of plywood. That was it. He didn't have anything else to send in the rest of the three-foot-square crate.

"Seems odd to ship an empty box," I ventured, before screwing down the top.

"Yeah," he said.

I looked around the warehouse for some heavy items. We threw in a bag of concrete, some broken pieces of cast-iron garden statuary, and a twenty-pound ingot of hard tar, then carried it to his trunk. It wouldn't fit all the way in.

I went to get some twine to tie the trunk lid down, and when I returned he said, "I'm a little low on bread, but I could pay you in hash if that would work for you."

"Yeah," I said. "That'll work for me." Since I wasn't paid anything from my dad, getting paid in hash was a good deal. Besides getting off the island, it was the only other thing I wanted.

He snapped the bar of hash in half and gave me some. It must have been about two ounces.

Just before he pulled away he said, "By the way, if you see a sailboat with red sails pull into the harbor, give me a call." He told me the name of his hotel.

"Sure," I replied. "I'll keep my eyes open."

As soon as he left I made a pipe out of some plumbing fittings and aluminum flashing. I got so high I passed out in the warehouse and slept on a sheet of packing foam.

A couple of days later I looked down at the harbor from our hillside house. There was a sailboat with rusty red sails reefed around the booms of the fore and aft masts. A red jib was set and the skipper was carefully trying to steer it toward the dock. The boat looked to be about fifty feet long, and every few minutes the skipper had to let go of the wheel at the stern, then dash to the jib to make an adjustment, then dash back to the wheel, then back to the jib. It was obviously a job for two men, and it was equally obvious that he was by himself. As the boat slowly picked its way through the moored yachts, I thought of Rik. Then, just before I went inside to call him on the phone, I took one more glance down at the boat and watched as it drifted head-on into the dock at the Hotel on the Cay. I could hear the faint thud as the bow hit the pilings.

After work I met Rik at the dock. We got in a dinghy and

rowed out to the boat. *Beaver* was painted across the stern. It was a sixty-foot gaff-rigged ketch with a wide beam—a real tub—but as I stood on deck it felt solid against the harbor chop. We were silently met by a tall well-tanned man wearing cutoff jeans and a T-shirt. He was British, and his name was Hamilton. I guessed he was forty years old, maybe fifty. He had a full beard, as bushy as a giant sea sponge, and intense blue eyes. He stood as still and meditative as a Greek Orthodox apostle. He didn't say a word, and as he looked me over, top to bottom, I felt like I'd been rubbed with sandpaper.

"We have a proposal to make," Rik said. I looked at Hamilton. He pursed his full lips and nodded.

"First," Rik continued, "before we get into the particulars, do you think you could help us sail this boat to New York, like, leave this week? And take, say, six weeks to deliver it?"

The thought of it hooked me right away and I was ready to push off immediately. That night, if necessary. With so much around me going the wrong way, I figured the boat was my exit. Plus, I'd end up in New York, where all the writers ended up.

"Yeah," I replied. "I can do that."

"Then here's the deal. But if you don't take it, you can't say a word to anyone."

"Okay," I said, glancing at Hamilton, who looked even more morose as he leaned over me.

"We have two thousand pounds of hash buried somewhere," Rik said. He pointed toward the ocean. "I need to fly to New York and arrange the deals, and we need someone, you, to help Hamilton sail the boat to Manhattan, where I'll be waiting. Your job is just to get the boat there, and for that you get ten thousand dollars. Cash. Of course, we can't pay you until we've made some deals, so you might have to stick around and help out a bit."

All I heard was the number—ten thousand dollars, cash. This was the jackpot. The answer I was looking for. My exit from St. Croix and my entrance to whatever good school would have me. I didn't think of the danger involved with breaking the law. I didn't even consider that I had no idea how to sail a large boat, or that Hamilton might kill me and dump my body off the coast of New Jersey—that *anything* bad could possibly happen. I just saw my exit from the island and entrance to my future, and it was glorious and good and calling me and there was no way I was going to get a better offer in a lifetime of sitting on St. Croix. And even if I had a good job it would take me years to save that kind of money. But now I could do it in six weeks and all for little work and lots of adventurous fun. I was ready. My heart was pounding.

"Count me in," I said, smiling. "I'll go home and start packing."

"Not a word to anyone about the cargo," Hamilton finally

said with his eyes bearing down on me. "No bragging to your friends. No loose talk. No *nothing*."

"Not a word," I replied earnestly. "I can keep a secret. You can trust me."

"I don't have a choice," he said, with some reluctance.

After that, there wasn't much to say. I was so anxious to get going I swam to shore and drove my car up the steep un-paved road to our house. All the way up I kept saying to my-self, "Now, settle down and think. Think about what you are doing. Be careful. Think about what you are risking." But I wasn't answering myself. I was so excited I knew I wasn't weighing the danger. I was ecstatic. I felt invulnerable. When I reached the top of the hill I looked down at the harbor. There was the sailboat floating on the blue water like a toy. My ship had come in, and I was ready to play.

The next day I told my mom and dad I'd been offered a sailing job, and had taken it and that I might be moving to New York.

"But you just got here," my mom said, disappointed.

"I can't blame you," Dad said. "If I could afford it, I'd get off this rock, too. Maybe the last crate I make will be my own—and hopefully it won't be a coffin." I hoped so, too.

I felt bad for him, but I had to go. Two days later he came down to the boat with me to look it over, and make sure it was seaworthy. He had been in the navy. I set it up in advance for

Hamilton not to be there and to just leave a note saying he was grocery shopping. I hadn't told Dad that Rik was involved. He already had him pegged, and I just knew if he laid eyes on Hamilton he'd peg him, too, and never let me go.

We spent about an hour looking over every square inch of the boat. I could tell Dad was on to something, but he couldn't quite put his finger on it. Finally he said, "Well, I guess this tub is shipshape." Then he looked me in the eye. "Is this on the up-and-up?" he asked.

"You bet," I replied.

"Then smooth sailing, sailor," he said, and slapped me on the back. "My only regret is that I'm not going with you."

I'm so glad he didn't.

2 / bon voyage

Before Hamilton and I set out on the final journey we took several practice voyages, and each one was disastrous in regard to seamanship and companionship. If I hadn't been so spellbound by the thought of ten thousand dollars in cash, I would have fled with the rats the moment the rust-colored sails were hoisted, because it was obvious that we didn't so much arrive at our destinations as aim and crash into them like kamikaze yachtsmen.

On our first practice run we couldn't even get out of the harbor without shaming ourselves in front of the entire boating community. We were in high spirits when we set off so we had the *Beaver* in full sail—the main and mizzen and jib smartly trimmed for all to see as we lumbered toward the channel through the reef which outlined the harbor. I was down in the main cabin opening a couple of cold beers for a mid-morning toast when a crash and a sudden pitch to starboard had me panicked. I could hear the brittle staghorn coral snapping off against our bow as the sail dragged us up and onto a reef. I dropped the beers and scrambled up the ladder to the main deck. Instead of steering between the port and starboard buoys marking the deep channel through the reef, Hamilton steered to the outside of the port marker. Now he stood at the wheel and scowled at me as if I had charted the course. "Don't just stand there," he barked, "lower the sails!" I hurried to get them down before we did any further damage to the hull. For all I knew we would sink. As I lowered the main, the keel struck a solid wall of coral heads and we heaved forward and came to a grinding stop. I flopped awkwardly onto the deck.

"Idiot!" Hamilton shouted. "Get up. You're making a fool of us."

"Don't blame me!" I snapped.

"Don't you dare talk back to the captain!" he snapped. "Now get to work." Then he went below and didn't return.

"Remember the money," I muttered angrily to myself. "The money. The money."

While I secured the sails I began to realize why he ducked out of sight. Boats passed out of the harbor and into the harbor and each one slowed to remark on my sailing gaffe and give me advice. It was clear that we had to sit there like wooden carrion until, if we were lucky, high tide would float us off. Four hours later, it did. Hamilton returned from below and I raised the sails.

"Take the wheel," Hamilton ordered, "and head for the Buck Island beach. I'm going to check the hull."

Buck Island was a small island just off the northeast coast of St. Croix. Before the racial trouble started, hundreds of tourists sunbathed there, and it was especially popular with scuba divers, who could follow an underwater park trail through the coral on the east side. Now, it was mostly deserted.

I aimed for the sandy west side. The wind was behind me and the mainsail was full out. The boat cruised along. Down below I could hear Hamilton knocking about, lifting boards and looking for leaks. It occurred to me that I knew nothing about survival at sea. The only commonsense facts I knew were to get in a life raft, have protection from the sun and plenty of fresh water, and drink your own urine when you run out of fresh water because saltwater will certainly kill you. My father had thought to teach me this after he had been in a sailing accident and stranded on a life raft for two days.

When Hamilton emerged he said the hull was fine, then checked the trim of the sails. He frowned at me as he pulled the main in a bit and tightened the jib. I just kept moving the wheel a little to the left and a little to the right, pretending that my small adjustments actually made a difference.

Hamilton stretched out on the deck and closed his eyes. "Wake me when we get there," he said.

I just stared at the huge mainsail and kept the wind behind us. I didn't want it to start luffing or Hamilton would hop up and get after me. In the few days we had spent outfitting the *Beaver*—checking the ropes, repairing sails, sealing the deck—he treated me like Billy Budd. I couldn't do anything right, and he just glowered at me like Claggart when I made a stupid mistake. I was thinking about what it was going to be like spending a month on board with only him when suddenly I noticed we were rapidly closing in on the island, and we were still under full sail.

"Hamilton!" I shouted. "Get up." I spun the wheel hard to port and began to lower the main. But it was too late. Our momentum took us directly toward the beach. We ran aground, softly, onto the sand. Only the bow was stuck, like a knife in a rum cake. A few locals ran toward us, laughing and shaking their heads in disbelief. We were the Keystone Kops of the sea. I waved back to them and grinned.

Hamilton was furious. "This is an outrage!" he said. "You've made a fool of us again!"

"Then keelhaul me!" I barked back.

"Don't tempt me," Hamilton said coldly. "Keelhauling is still legal in the British navy." Then he ducked down the hatch and in a minute the motor started and he shifted the boat into reverse. The sea beneath our stern bubbled up but the screw didn't generate enough torque to pull us out. Finally, one of the idle tourist boats edged up alongside our stern and the captain tossed me a lanyard. I tied it to a cleat and he towed us off the beach.

"Thanks," I shouted when we had been set loose. I untied the lanyard and let it drop to the water.

"Anytime," the skipper called back, and I could make out his sly smile as he deftly coiled the rope.

Two days later we left St. Croix for good. We set out at night in calm water with our lights off and followed the channel markers north out of the harbor, past Buck Island, and farther, toward St. John and Virgin Gorda. When I turned to say good-bye to St. Croix I could see two warehouses burning down at the docks. The white exodus was even more frantic now. Already those who could see the writing on the wall were torching their own property for the insurance money before it became worthless. The flames illuminated a small city of wooden crates that had already been packed with personal goods and prepared for shipping.

But I was filled with joy and triumph, and the fires to me were the flames of Troy still burning as Odysseus pushed off for Ithaca. I was ready for adventure.

It was not lost on me that so many writers had gone to sea, and for them, setting off to cross the water was the same as setting down to fill the pages with their adventures. Before leaving I had gone to a used bookstore and selected every title I could find which had something to do with the sea. I had *Billy Budd, Martin Eden, Treasure Island, Heart of Darkness, The Odyssey, Robinson Crusoe,* and the *Mutiny on the Bounty* trilogy. I was armed with books the way the navy goes to sea armed to the teeth. I figured these books would have to live with me as cabin companions since Hamilton was so snappish. But I didn't mind. I wanted to write while sailing, and I was more than willing to come under the spell of books.

All through the first night Hamilton took the wheel because only he knew where the hash was buried. At dawn I was asleep in the aft cabin when suddenly I was thrown out of my bunk and onto the floor. I could hear Hamilton cursing on deck. The ropes were slapping the mast and the boom was tangled in the stanchion ropes. I slipped on my Top-Siders and went up. By then Hamilton had the gaff and boom under control and I pulled down the jib.

"What happened?" I yelled into the wind.

"Riptide," he hollered back. "Not to worry."

Riptide my ass, I thought. I figured he had fallen asleep but wouldn't admit it. I looked around. We had rolled up against a menacing chain of sharp rocks that stuck out of the ocean like a shark's lower jaw. Hamilton started the engine and as we backed away I could see we were in a beautiful spot.

It seemed to me to be the most wonderful sight I had ever seen. The rising sun was buttering the clouds, the sea was royal blue, and dolphins darted in and out of the water, weaving between the rocks with absolute grace. Finally, I thought, something good has happened. Maybe our luck will change.

Off the starboard side, now about a hundred yards away, was a small, uninhabited island no more than five acres. It was made of immense granite slabs each one the size of a train car and all piled up as if derailed. In each crack grew a gnarly sea grape tree deformed from leeward winds. And at the water's edge was a perfect melon slice of a beach all protected by the outer chain of sharp rocks.

"It's called Little Dog Island," Hamilton said. "I got us here, now you get the dinghy and go ashore. Somewhere beneath that stand of trees you'll find a tarp covered with sand. Under that is the hash. Start bringing it on board—but don't get it wet."

"Fine," I said. But inside I was dancing around to a pirate jig. "Yo-ho-ho," I sang in my belly, imagining myself as Long John Silver about to put to shore. "Fifteen men on the dead man's chest! Yo-ho-ho and a bottle of rum. Drink and devil had done the rest. Yo-ho-ho and a bottle of rum!"

I never would have made a good pirate like Billy Bones or Black Dog. I didn't have the stamina. I dug up the canvas bags—each weighing fifty pounds—dragged them through the sand, loaded four at a time into the dinghy, rowed through the choppy surf and out through the rocks to the *Beaver*, tied up, precariously balanced on the dinghy gunnels while heaving each sack on deck. I did this ten times in a row, until finally, when I had finished lugging the two thousand pounds of hash on board and had hauled up the dinghy and secured it to its cradle, I dropped down onto the deck and lay there as if I had fallen from the top of the mast. I was exhausted.

Hamilton had been packing the bags in the fo'c'sle, in his cabin, and in mine, and wasn't nearly as tired. "Grog time!" he hollered from down below, and rang a brass bell. I forced myself to stand and staggered down the ladder into the main cabin and over to the galley door. "Here you go, sailor," he said, suddenly full of good captainly cheer, then poured me a tumbler of rum and locked the bottle away.

I drank it straight back and asked for more.

"British navy rules," he replied. "Only one grog per day per man."

"Are you serious?" I asked.

"Sailor, this is serious business," he replied, underlining each word with his tone. "I can't have any drunks on board."

"Aye, aye, captain," I said sarcastically.

I never did get drunk, but I got after the hash like a mouse at cheese. I nibbled on it each day—a gram here and a gram there. Hamilton took his hash in tea—the British way, I assumed. He shaved his down to a powder with a straight edge razor then dipped a heaping spoonful into a cup of hot water and stirred it up with sugar. Stoned out of our minds, we navigated through the long madhouse days of the voyage as if crossing the ocean in a floating sanitarium. I spent hours sitting cross-legged on deck with the ship's log on my lap recording the day's events as if I were drifting around in Baudelaire's *Artificial Paradise*.

The ship was a strange floating cell. A blue cell. Blue sky. Blue ocean. We weren't locked in, but there was nowhere to go, and aside from the weather, each day unfolded very much the same. Bright, blinding blue. What changed was the drama on board. Hamilton was insane. Or so I thought. He wouldn't talk to me, except to order me around or humiliate me in some way. He stopped wearing clothes. He constantly paced the deck in the nude, staring out at the horizon line and stroking his beard. He must have been thinking about something because the moods on his face were as shifty as the clouds overhead. He whispered things I couldn't make out. He counted numbers on his fingers as if he were making lists. For hours he practiced tying and untying knots. At times he looked at me as if he had never seen me before.

We had two bunks, a toilet, a galley, no radio, plenty of books, a deck of cards, a chess set, and two thousand pounds of hash. After we had loaded the hash at Little Dog Island I began snooping around the boat, just to see what else I could find. I lifted the cushioned lid of a galley bench and inside were all sorts of sailing gear: flags for half a dozen countries, a rusty flare gun (which made me think of Rik's forehead), a fire extinguisher, rain slickers, and a book the size of a dictionary. It was clothbound in green linen, and embossed in gold on the cover was the name of the ship. I set it on the galley table and opened the cover. It was blank. Dozens of pages had been ripped out. The remaining pages were wrinkled and stained from water damage. It smelled salty, and a bit like diesel fuel. I loved it, and immediately thought it was up to me to record my boat's history, like so many other sea writers had done. I turned the page, smoothed it out with my hand, and got started.

3 / ship's log

July 15: Today I took a photograph of Hamilton sitting at the wheel with the sun setting behind him. He frowned. "Now take a picture of me," I said, and handed him the camera.

He flipped the camera over, unsnapped the back, pulled out the film, and tossed it over his shoulder into the ocean. "If I find any more film on board it will join that roll," he said.

"It's just a photo," I replied.

"It's evidence," he snapped back. This is the first evidence I have had that he even thinks we could be caught.

"Let me see your wallet," he said.

I gave it to him.

He threw away all my identification except for my fake Florida license. "Might come in handy," he said.

July 16: Dead calm today. Hot. The sails hanging limply from the gaffs like sleeping bats. At one point I dove overboard and swam around the boat as if it were at anchor. Hamilton threw an empty bottle overboard and we bobbed along next to it for hours. By the end of the day we may have covered a mile. No more. Feel like a sitting duck. Said so to Hamilton. He drifted into a story about his biggest concern on the ocean being pirates, not police. Told me about friends *in the business* who were boarded by pirates who tied them to the masts, and then took their stash. Somehow I find this absurd and can't stop thinking of Captain Hook and his crew of pirates in *Peter Pan*. Wish Hamilton would swallow a clock so I could hear him creeping around. He stalks me like a mumbling crocodile.

July 17: Started reading *Heart of Darkness*. Already thinking that Kurtz is waiting for me in New York along with his gang of savages—and a deep mystery about the evil in the soul of man that I can't solve until I get there.

July 18: Woke up to gunshots. Carefully stuck my head above the deck hatch and saw Hamilton firing his pistol at cans he tossed into the air. He missed them all. I knew he had a pistol because I'd poked around the cabin and found it under his mattress. When he saw me he made me put a can on the end of a yardstick and stand up on the bow while he shot at it from the stern. He missed each time, which was not a relief. I heard the bullets whiz by. William Tell was a good shot and put an arrow through an apple on his son's head. William Burroughs was a terrible shot. He put a glass of water on his wife's head and shot her just above the eye. The Mexican police called her death an accident. If Hamilton hit me I'd just drop into the water and sink like a stone. Nobody would know the difference— not even him.

July 19: I've missed talking to another human. Last night, after Hamilton came to relieve me of my shift, instead of heading down to the main cabin to sleep, I stayed put. I remained as mute as Friday to Crusoe, hoping that he'd break the ice. But he didn't. He held his hot tea to his lips, and patted delicately at his beard, his fingers slowly adjusting the symmetry after his nap.

"Have you ever thought about what might happen to us if we get caught?"

Hamilton's laugh came out of him like a coiled spring jigging up and down. He had to set down his teacup.

"You are *afraid*," he finally said. "Afraid of the punishment. You can't be afraid of what we are doing, because we're doing nothing wrong."

My fear amused him. He began a new round of wild laughter. The compass light illuminated his face so that he looked like a carved pumpkin. If I had any hope of reaching shore, I'd jump overboard.

I stood up and went downstairs. But I didn't sleep. Hamilton had read my mind—I'm not doing anything wrong. I'm just afraid of the punishment.

July 20: The sea is like unrolled velvet under the half moon. Fell asleep at my watch. Tilted forward and hit the edge of the compass with my chin. Blood streamed down my neck and chest. Thought I had severed my carotid artery. When Hamilton saw me he shook his head. After he had a cup of tea he cleaned out the gash and put a bandage on it. I should be fine. Had a headache all day.

July 21: No birds. No music. No noise. No clouds. No wind. Hamilton pacing in circles like an angry clock. In the sky the jet streams crisscross from east to west and west to east like ICBMs. Perhaps when we reach New York it won't be there. No city. No country. No people. We'll just travel around the globe like the navy in Nevil Shute's *On the Beach,* searching for survivors and waiting for the radiation cloud to cook us.

July 22: Ate too much hash. Stared up at the full moon's blemished face. Thought of men walking on the moon. During the first moon walk I was watching television at a friend's house in Florida when a car ran off the road and hit the side of the house. Scared the crap out of us. The man had been driving with his head sticking out the window, staring up at the moon, looking to see the spaceship.

July 23: Not well.

July 24: Same as yesterday.

July 25: I was sitting at the cabin table eating some dried prunes when Hamilton looked over at me from the kitchen. "I haven't seen you take a shit yet," he remarked.

"So?" I replied. My face reddened. Taking a shit was private business.

"Just curious," he said. "It's a small boat. If you don't shit in the crapper I can only hope you're not doing it like a sneaky cat behind the hash."

"Well, I'm not shitting in the fo'c'sle, if that's what you mean."

"Where then?" he asked, raising his nose like a shit detective and sniffing loudly.

"Overboard," I said. "Like the old-time sailors."

"Those old-timers had seats out under the bowsprit. What do you do? Just hang off the bowsprit and shit down the back of your legs?"

"No. I jump into the water and hang on to the towrope and shit in the ocean."

"Bloody hell!" he cried out.

"Bloody hell!" I cried back, mocking him.

"You know what can happen to your ass if you shit in the sea?"

"Get arrested by Jacques Cousteau?"

"No. Worse. You can get your ass bit off. Sharks will chum your links and bite your arse down to the bone."

"You're putting me on," I said.

"Seen it happen," he said. "A fellow named Guy went to fertilize the sea and after he did his duty a shark took his legs."

"Really?"

"Believe it," he said.

"So how do you do it?" I asked.

"The crapper," he said. "That's what it's there for."

"Are you telling the truth?" I asked.

"Of course," he said. "I still need help sailing the boat otherwise I wouldn't give a shit about your ass."

July 26: Started using the crapper.

July 27: All the bread is old. Furry with medallions of blue mold. Hamilton toasts it. Each time we take a bite clouds of mold spores drift across the table. We slather the bread with jam in an effort to keep the dust in place. It helps, but as soon as the bread splits open it coughs out another cloud. We have to eat it on deck with the wind to our backs to keep ourselves from gagging.

July 29: Another night without a breeze. Nothing to do. I tried to read, but instead of focusing my attention I became restless. I'm tired of just sitting. I smoked some hash and then dove overboard. I swam around the boat and on my second lap I noticed Hamilton's porthole was open. We usually keep them closed, but with the sea so flat we aren't worried about waves splashing through. I stopped beneath the porthole and listened for a minute. I could hear him breathing, heavily. I held on to the bottom rim of the hole and pulled myself up with one hand. With the other I reached in and grabbed his leg. He hollered, and kicked out.

I dropped under the water, but even from there I could hear the gunshot.

Oh no, I thought. I flipped him out. I swam around to the stern and pulled myself up. As soon as I got my head above the deck I saw him step up out of the main hatch and point the pistol at me. It went off. I buckled and dropped back into the water. I was so scared I didn't know if he had shot me or not. I swam around to the port side and quietly broke the surface. I reached up and held on to the bottom of a stanchion. I could hear Hamilton back at the stern.

"You think you're so funny? I'll show you what scared is!" He fired into the water. And again. "You laughing yet? You failed to consider that in the British navy an officer has the right to execute a sailor who is a danger to an operation."

I didn't know how to calm him down so I kept quiet. I peeked up over the deck and watched him. After a few minutes he dropped the gun and began to adjust the sails.

"Here we are," he shouted to himself, "bobbing out here like a bloody cork. It's enough to make a man go mad and I'm stuck here with a nitwit."

I dropped back into the water and swam around to the stern, where it was easier to pull myself up. "Can I come aboard, captain?" I asked.

"Yes," he said. "I'm tired of wanting to shoot you. I'd just like to flog you instead." Then he turned and went back to his cabin. I retook the wheel and when my shift was up I didn't dare go wake him. And when he finally came to relieve me, he didn't say a word. He certainly scared me. And I think he scared himself firing blindly into the water. I didn't like that he called me a nitwit, but I haven't brought it up for discussion.

July 30: Of all the sea books I've been reading, the book that has taken me over is Jack London's *Martin Eden*. Just as Holden

Caulfield sees phonies everywhere, those same phonies can't recognize Eden's talent and they run him down. He was a man trying to create greatness, and the phonies were too ignorant to recognize anything beyond their own limitations.

On my night shift I've begun to act out the final scene, where Martin Eden pushes himself through a porthole and dives into the dark water and intentionally drowns himself. I don't have a porthole to dive through, but I do have a ship to dive from. I don't really want to kill myself so I tie the end of our yellow towline in a tight knot around my ankle before diving in. There in the darkness with the sky full of stars I lie on my back and glide through the water with the boat pulling me along. It is beautiful to look at the boat, lit only by the compass light and the moon off the sails as she glides up and over the slow swells. It is so peaceful. Martin had once seen the moon as hopeful, too, but after he was beaten down by cynics the moon was dark for him. I wondered if I could ever kill myself as he had. If that yellow towline slipped off my foot, would I sink into the sea as he had or would I swim for all my life to catch up to it? I won't know until it happens. I do know that there is no reason for me to drown myself from sorrow since I haven't yet tried to achieve anything great.

July 31: For the last week the wind has been unusually calm, and in order to make any time at all we have lowered the sails and used the engine. Soon, we speculate, we will run out of fuel. About midday I saw in the distance what I first thought was an oil derrick. I pointed it out to Hamilton. "Let's take a look," he said.

We coursed toward it. Oddly, we couldn't seem to hold our bearing and the rig kept moving from our port side to starboard.

"Is something wrong with our rudder?" I asked. I was worried because the great German battleship *Bismarck* had been hit in the rudder and was doomed to going in circles until she was sunk by the British. If Hamilton and I were stuck going in circles, we'd soon try to kill each other—and I'd be the one getting torpedoed.

Hamilton fiddled with the wheel. "No, we're fine," he replied.

Then, as we got closer, we figured it out. It wasn't an oil derrick but an enormous Japanese fishing trawler with two tall cranes for hauling up their vast nets. Hamilton had seen one before. "They stay out for a year at a time," he said. "They catch the fish, then process and can them right on board. It's a floating factory."

I went up to the bow and began to wave to them. I could see that they were trying to avoid us because they didn't want us to foul their nets, and now the large cranes were hauling them up. A few fish flopped around trying to get back to the sea.

"Ahoy!" I shouted through my cupped hands. "Do you speak English?"

The rail was lined with ragged Japanese sailors waving down at me. The deck must have been thirty feet up. After a few minutes they found a sailor who knew English.

"We're low on fuel," I hollered. "Do you have extra?"

"Yes," he hollered back. In a moment a rope ladder was lowered.

"Put some pants on," I said to Hamilton.

"Mind your own business, sailor," he replied.

I dove overboard and swam to the ladder and climbed up.

The captain greeted me. Through the interpreter he ordered several men to fetch the fuel. They brought back five-gallon cans and lowered them down to Hamilton, who had pulled in close. He filled our tank.

I said thank you and climbed down the ladder. When I got on our deck Hamilton gave me a bottle of rum to take back up as a thank-you gift. I climbed the ladder and presented the bottle to the captain. He took it, bowed politely, then fired off some orders. A man went running to the bridge and in a moment returned with a giant bottle of sake. It was as tall and round as decorative bottles they use in liquor store displays and I had to use both hands to carry it. I bowed low to the captain, then looked down the ladder. I didn't think I could climb it without using my hands. Hamilton had drifted off about twenty yards so I just backed up a few steps, held the bottle up over my head and screamed as I ran and jumped.

The ship was a lot higher than I figured. As I hugged the bottle against my chest I tilted forward. And when I hit the water the bottle knocked the wind clear out of me. I couldn't breathe, and I kept sinking. I could see the bottom of the ship and the small fish swimming alongside the bilge drains. I thought of Martin Eden sinking lower and lower, forcing himself deeper and deeper. I thought of Jack London not putting a final period on the last sentence of the book as Martin lost consciousness and drifted into death. But I didn't want to die. I held the neck of the bottle with my left hand and began to swim toward the surface. My lungs were burning. I bit down on my lip to keep from taking in a mouthful of water. I kept kicking and stroking my arm overhead until I broke the surface and sucked in a lungful of air. I was almost dead, and now I was alive again. It was glorious. I turned onto my back and floated with the sake on my belly. The Japanese cheered from the deck and I rolled over and with one arm dog-paddled my way to the *Beaver*, where I grabbed the towline and held on. Hamilton reeled me in and I held up the sake. "This is mine," I said.

He took it from me. "You earned it, sailor," he said. Then he reached out and gave me a hand getting up over the stern.

"I thought you were dead," he remarked, finally smiling at me.

"Me, too. It was great."

I waved to the Japanese, then unscrewed the cap and took a big swig and poured it over my face. They roared their approval. Hamilton started the engine and we motored west, looking for land.

August 1: Now that we have fuel we have been going all out and our spirits are high. We are both looking forward to land. After a day of smooth sailing the water has turned choppy and looks to get worse. The sky is low and pressing down on us. The temperature has dropped. Hamilton put on pants and a shirt. The weather has been easy so we might be getting close to Cape Hatteras (we think), where there is always rough weather. But we don't know our exact position. We have no ship-to-shore radio. The sextant is broken because I was playing with it and snapped off a piece. I didn't tell Hamilton. We have no radio directional finder, just the compass. All along we have been headed roughly north by northwest and figure once we hit land we'll just follow the coast up.

August 2: By this morning the wind picked up and the waves broke over the bow and swept across the deck, over the cabin, and all the way back to the stern, where either Hamilton or I was tethered to the wheel with a rope around our chest. The constant pounding of the waves is so exhausting we have to change shifts every hour. Tonight it is pitch-black except for the light from the cabin windows. We have the sails tightly reefed and tied down. If it weren't for the extra fuel the Japanese gave us, we'd be trying to steady ourselves with the jib—which seems impossible. I think we would be swamped by now.

August 3 and 4: Storm.

August 5: After three full days and nights of the storm we are exhausted and have no idea of our position.

I was on watch this morning when a Coast Guard turbo-prop passed low overhead and circled around and dipped low over us again.

Hamilton heard it and stuck his head out of the main hatch.

"What's he up to?" I asked.

"They're just scanning the water after the storm," Hamilton said. "Making sure there's no trouble. Must mean we're close to land."

With the next pass of the turboprop it was so low we could feel the prop wash. I waved to the captain, he waved back, then curled to the west.

"Follow that plane," Hamilton ordered. "I bet he's heading back to the base."

We got a compass reading on the plane before it disappeared. That night we spotted lights on the coast, but still didn't know our exact location. We stayed offshore, following the lights north, and figured in the morning we'd locate an inlet where we might find a marina and rest up for a few days.

August 6: This morning the weather was hazy with low visibility. We could hear more activity across the water than what we could see, so we knew we were close to something. Then as the haze lifted we saw a sign announcing that we were in restricted military waters.

"Bloody hell," Hamilton cursed. "Let's just push on until someone tells us to turn around."

"Can't we just turn around now?" I asked. "Why invite trouble?"

"Just do as you're told," he snapped. "Take the bow and keep a look out for shallow water."

I did. The water was all slate gray on the surface and I couldn't tell if it was twenty feet deep or two. Suddenly I heard a motorboat coming our way, and as it pulled close enough I could see it was a small Coast Guard launch. Hamilton saw it, too.

"What do we do?" I asked.

"Wave nicely," he said. I could see the outline of the gun in his pocket.

Don't do anything stupid, I thought, as I waved and

smiled. They kept getting closer. Finally they pulled up within five feet of our port side.

"You have entered restricted waters," shouted a cadet through a bullhorn. "Turn starboard and we'll escort you out."

"Where are we?" I asked.

"Cape May, New Jersey," the cadet shouted. "Home of the Coast Guard training base."

"Oh, sweet Jesus," I muttered. "We're dead."

I must have gone pale. The cadet laughed through the bullhorn, which made him seem as sinister as Poseidon was with Odysseus when he kept foiling his attempts to get home to Ithaca.

Hamilton turned north and we followed them across the inlet. The entire time I was waiting for them to pull us over and do a customs check. Hamilton insisted on flying the British Union Jack. He thought it made us look friendly and less suspicious, but in doing so it left us open for a customs check by any military and police patrol boat.

Before long we began to spot signs for gas stations and boating supplies, and along the shore there were white mooring buoys. We were back in civilian waters when suddenly we came to an abrupt stop and I toppled onto the deck. We had run aground again.

"Are you okay?" the cadet called over as I hopped to my feet. "Need a tow out?"

"No," I shouted back. "We're just going to stop here for a while. We'll be fine."

"Suit yourself," he said, waved, and the launch turned and sped away. My heart was pounding.

"That was a close call," I said.

"The worst thing about you is you always look so guilty. If you want to be any good at this business you've got to learn to relax. Now, throw out the anchor and get the dinghy ready," Hamilton ordered. "We're going to shore."

When we got off in Cape May it was the first time in three weeks I had been on land, and I had sea legs. I walked like a drunken elephant stumping from side to side. We found a burger place and bought hot food and cold drinks. Better yet, I went into the bathroom. I hadn't had a freshwater bath in three weeks and was glistening with caked salt like a stick of rock crystal candy. I splashed cold, fresh water on my face. It felt so good.

All day we tried to reach Rik. He is staying at the Chelsea Hotel in Manhattan. They have him registered, but haven't seen him in days. I asked Hamilton where he met Rik. "At a smugglers' convention," he said sarcastically.

There is nothing left to do but push on.

4 / i love new york

Everyone in prison has a story about how They were caught.
Sitting on the edge of a man's bunk while telling and listening
to stories about how people got busted is about the same as being in the Boy Scouts and sitting around a campfire telling
ghost stories. Being scared together created a great bond
among boys, and being scared of each other created a great
bond in prison. Most of the time individuality was measured
by how violent you could be, and this kept everyone on edge.
But what we all had in common, and what everyone liked to
share, is how we got caught.

I loved those getting-caught stories, and they were among
the first ones I wrote down in my secret prison journal. They
had what every story should have: action running like a fleeing suspect across the surface shadowed step for step by big
risks and big emotions. Of course they always ended about the
same. Guys either turned themselves in, were taken by sur-
prise, or were taken by force. But every one of them felt it dif-

ferently, and did their time their own way—everything from "hard" time to "standing on their head."

Since about half of the guys in prison were in for bank robbery, I heard a lot of their stories. I met an ex–Green Beret who robbed banks. He was running around with another man's wife and she got tired of him. So to get rid of him she had him rob a string of banks and hide the money with her. Then she called the FBI and turned him in. There was a Chinese man who didn't speak much English and couldn't read it. He was in for bank robbery, too. His claim was that he was waiting for a bus when a man pulled up in a car and offered him twenty bucks to run into the corner bank and hand a teller a note, then return with the package. He did what he was told. It was a stick-up note. The teller gave the Chinese guy a bag of cash, he gave it to the guy in the car, and soon after he was arrested while still waiting for his bus. One guy claimed he was narcoleptic. He handed the teller the stick-up note, and then became so tense he passed out and woke up in custody. And then there were the usual ones—drug addicts who robbed banks to keep up their habits and were finally caught in the act. They didn't wear masks, they didn't even own cars, they didn't get but a few thousand dollars each time—they were just playing a game of cops and robbers until they were caught. A lot of those guys had more friends and relatives in prison than out. Then there were the ones who shot bystanders and cops, their partner, or, by accident, themselves. A guy named Moon had dropped his gun and shot himself in the eye. I took his X-ray, and the .22 slug was clear as day in his frontal lobe. Another guy shot himself in the leg. The bone never healed properly. An infection spiked up and he was rushed to the emergency room downtown where a two-inch section of his tibia and fibula was removed.

Of course we had the usual list of guys in for car theft, pimping, mail theft, murder, manslaughter, assault, burglary, larceny, arson, explosives, drug possession, drug dealing. And me, in for smuggling. This is how I got caught.

After our stopover in Cape May we came right up the New Jersey coast. By that evening I could see the lights shining brightly on the Statue of Liberty. She was like a lookout waving her arm and giving us the all-clear. Behind her, the skyscrapers of New York waited for us like a crowd held back, straining, ready to pounce. But were they a crowd of buyers, or police? I stood on the bow and looked through the binoculars. I didn't know what I was looking for, but I can tell you the fear of waiting to get caught was worse than getting caught. Every boat I saw, every noise I heard, every helicopter that spanked through the air, every searchlight that spun its bright eye toward us made me jump.

Would the police be expecting us? Would they come at us

101

with a police launch? Or would they just take their time and wait for us to start selling? I scanned the water, the coastline, and the air. I knew they were watching us. Still, there was nothing to do but go forward and hope that Rik had made arrangements to sell the hash.

"Are you worried?" Hamilton asked.

"Yes," I said. "I'll be worried until it's all over."

He laughed. "The police aren't that smart. My greatest fear is a snitch. That's always the weak link. The police are too stupid to catch you on their own. Every fat-assed bobby in the world depends on his snitch to do the dirty work."

I wasn't in the mood to hear it. I was creeped out of my skin and waiting for a cop to reach up over the stern and yell, "Gotcha!" I returned to the bow and put on a life vest. I was a strong swimmer. I figured I could dive overboard and make my way to Miss Liberty. I raised my binoculars to my eyes. If the cops were coming, I wanted to see them first.

Since we hadn't hooked up with Rik, we didn't have a dock space reserved for us. Hamilton figured we'd just cruise around until we found something that looked available, but as it grew darker it was difficult to spot any marina space. We went up the oil-slicked East River, under the Brooklyn Bridge and along the east side of Manhattan. Along the way sailors waved to us. I thought they had seen the British Union Jack and were friendly. In return, Hamilton gave them his royal wave as if he were the queen of England, and I waved as if I were riding a homecoming float. What I didn't know is that the East River was closed to pleasure craft traffic, which is why we were being waved away. But no police launch pulled us over. We passed by La Guardia Airport, with the jets soaring above our heads and the hot breath of their engines rolling down over us.

We made it all the way up to Queens before spotting a lighted marina sign. Hamilton headed toward the orange bumpers at the end of the dock.

"Should I drop an anchor?" I asked, and prepared to throw one over to slow us down.

"No," he ordered. "Just take a line and jump on the dock and catch a cleat."

As the boat evened up with the end of the dock I jumped off and hooked a line around a cleat, but the wood was rotted and the cleat bolts ripped out of the dock. I tried to haul the boat around, but it was a losing cause and finally I had to drop the line before being pulled into the water.

"Bloody incompetent!" Hamilton cursed and drifted onward until the bowsprit speared a metal barge. The barge was empty, and from the blow it sounded as if our arrival to Flushing had been announced with a Chinese gong. It brought the marina manager out of his little shed. Hamilton reversed the engine and sputtered back to where I could leap aboard, grab the line, and leap back onto the dock, where I looped it around a solid piling head and pulled it snug.

We made arrangements to keep the boat there. It seemed pretty remote and we felt secure being so out of the way. We walked up the dark street to a pay phone and Hamilton called Rik. He was in his room and ready to start moving the hash. He had a car, and had set up a two-hundred-and-fifty-pound sale. That news cheered me up and I didn't feel so gloomy anymore. Maybe, I thought, all that sitting around on the boat was making me paranoid. Maybe I should just relax and go with the flow.

On the way back to the boat I went into a little store and bought a case of cold beer and some food. As soon as I popped a beer open I began to feel better. We had the boat tied up. We hadn't been caught on the way in. And now that the selling had begun, the money would be flowing. I'd be paid and on my way to picking a new college.

When we got back on board, Hamilton used an old bathroom scale to weigh out the kilos of hash. I packed them in the canvas bags. When Rik arrived we threw the hash in the trunk and took off with Hamilton driving like a madman.

"Stick with the speed limit," Rik reminded him. "We don't want to get pulled over."

"Nonsense," Hamilton said. "I used to be a professional driver in Manchester. I know what to do."

"Hey, Rik," I butted in. "Did you get the crate okay?"

"Yeah," he said, unfolding a map. "No problem, except for getting the screws out." I smiled. I had used extra-long ones.

We were heading for Woodstock, New York, about ninety miles away. There was a guy named Jerome who would meet us at some gas station and we'd follow him to his place in the woods.

Jerome was waiting for us in his psychedelic hippie van, which was decorated with Day-Glo Peter Max designs. He might as well have had a neon sign saying "We have drugs! Arrest Us Now!" He made me nervous. We followed him down a dirt road into the country and came to a small shingled house. There was something wrong with it. It was off center, like something out of a fairy tale. "Built it myself," Jerome said proudly, hooking his thumbs into the front of his jeans. He recited the Crooked Man nursery rhyme, and grinned. We all smiled politely. I thought he was retarded in some way. I figured a person could not invent himself into a "Crooked Jerome," but had to be born that way.

Jerome's money connection hadn't arrived and nobody knew why, especially Jerome. He made a few calls from his crooked wall phone and kept assuring us the guy was coming. "It's legit!" he said, and pulled nervously on his long black beard as if it were black taffy. "I swear. It's legit."

So we waited, and waited, and waited, until we thought

the deal was crooked. But Jerome convinced us to spend the night. I was suspicious. His house was crooked, he might be, too. Maybe he was as crazed as Charlie Manson and would kill us in our sleep. I was getting paranoid—not about the drugs, but about the people who used the drugs.

In the middle of the night I woke up on the couch. It was pitch-black. I staggered across the uneven floor and caromed off the walls and furniture. I spotted a sliver of moon through a window. That was good enough for me. I climbed out and staggered off into the bushes until I figured I was lost and nobody could find me, even if they wanted to drive a twelve-inch knife into my belly. I sat down against a tree and fell asleep. The next morning no one seemed to be out looking for me so I sneaked up on the house fully expecting to find a bloodbath. Instead, everyone was up and smoking hash for breakfast. I was tired of that. I smoked a cigarette and had a cup of coffee. Not long after, Jerome's friend arrived with the money and we were all relieved and happy as we counted out the cash.

On the way back to New York we got caught in a thunderstorm. The rain was blinding. The traffic slowed to a crawl. Hamilton kept checking the rearview mirror.

"What's up?" I asked.

"We're being followed," he replied, and abruptly turned the wheel. We went off the road and slid into the grassy median. Already the rainwater had collected and we sped like a ski boat down the swale. I was frozen with panic. We couldn't see a thing but sheets of water rushing over us as if we were a sinking ship. I kept thinking we were going to hit a bridge abutment and flatten up like a smashed beer can. We wouldn't be arrested. We'd be buried.

"Slow down," Rik said. "No one is following us."

"Bloody hell if they aren't," Hamilton spit back. "The same car that followed us up to Jerome's is behind us again. When we pulled into the gas station to meet Jerome yesterday, it pulled in behind us."

"Why didn't you say something?" Rik asked.

"Didn't know if we were being tagged until just now," he said.

Hamilton kept plowing through the water and when the rain lightened he veered up the side of the median and screeched back onto the highway and kept going. "I think we lost them," he said, and smiled thinly as he patted his beard into shape.

"You're paranoid," Rik said. "There was nobody back there."

"Bloody hell" is all Hamilton said then, and "Bloody hell," he said more viciously when we returned to the marina. As soon as we parked the car the manager came running toward us.

"Just to let you know," he said breathlessly, "during the

storm your boat broke away from the dock. I was going to go pull it in, but before I could do so two men came up in a launch and boarded her. They tied her back up and I think they threw another anchor over, too. Were they friends of yours?"

At that moment I knew my fears were real. We were doomed. The extra anchor was in the fo'c'sle next to five hundred pounds of hash. Whoever got that anchor knew what we were doing. Something was up, and I could only think it would get worse. I started looking around the marina to see if I could spot the cops.

"Thanks," Hamilton said coolly to the marina owner, and we pulled back over to the street.

"Rik," Hamilton ordered, "you take the cash and car back to the hotel. Jack, you and I will move the boat. Let's go."

And just like that I was walking toward the dock, knowing for certain now that someone was watching us. Someone knew. And it had to be the police. I felt like Henry Fleming going into battle for the second time. I was afraid, but something inside me had already accepted that I would be caught, just as he had accepted his death.

"They probably saw the hash next to the anchor," I whispered to Hamilton.

"They may not know what it is," he replied. "Once I got caught with forty pounds of hash in my suitcase and I told the customs agent it was hair henna from Egypt and he let me pass. They aren't that smart."

Maybe they were stupid, I thought to myself. But not that stupid. We boarded the boat and snooped around.

"Perhaps they were just decent people helping out," Hamilton said. "Now pull up the anchor and cast us off from the dock—quietly. I want to drift for a while and see if we attract any friends. And remember, if anyone boards us, just play innocent. I'll tell them we're stealing the boat. The worst that can happen is we'll be busted for theft."

"They won't fall for that," I said, and instinctively looked over my shoulder and stared into the dark buildings and boats. I could feel someone's eyes on me. I just couldn't see them.

"You always act so guilty," Hamilton said derisively. "You attract bad vibes. Now, pull the anchor."

I pulled the anchor and we drifted across the marina's basin in the rain until Hamilton was satisfied that no one was following. Then we started the engine and motored down the inky East River with the tall, checkered buildings blinking down at us. I stared back at them, and felt as Marlowe had, searching the shoreline for Kurtz in Conrad's *Heart of Darkness*. At one point a large barge nearly brushed up against us and I imagined we would be boarded by cannibals. Finally, we rounded the tip of Manhattan and steered up the Hudson where, without incident, we docked at the 79th Street Marina. Maybe our sailing luck was changing, I thought. Maybe Hamilton is right—I'm just paranoid. After we tied up and Hamilton advanced the marina operator some cash to look after things, we caught a cab to the Chelsea Hotel.

"I told you not to worry," Hamilton said, satisfied with himself as he caressed his beard. "They aren't that smart."

"I'll breathe a lot easier when I have my money and I'm out of here," I said.

"Relax," he said. "You're bumming me out."

The next day and all throughout the week Rik worked the telephone and kept records of sales and contacts. Between delivering the hash around town, I sat around the bizarre lobby at the Chelsea, smoked hash, and updated the ship's log. The art hanging, or leaning, against the hotel walls was so odd, so weird, so impossible to understand. I felt trapped by an intense ignorance. I couldn't tell what was hip and what was hideous, or what was sane or insane. Plus, the lobby seemed a spiderweb of trapped psychotic poets and artists. Or so I guessed. Which ones were the real artists and which ones were the poseurs? Who did I want to meet? Who did I want to avoid? Perhaps they were just street people who had wandered in to flop down in the beat-up chairs and smoke pot or shoot up in the elevator. When I asked Rik his opinion of them he told me they were Andy Warhol's movie-star friends.

"Ever see *Chelsea Girls*?" he asked.

I hadn't. Had never heard of it.

"Well, half the cast is down there," he said. "You ought to introduce yourself to them. Maybe you'll get into one of his films."

I was too shy for that.

"I thought I saw Dennis Hopper down there the other day," he said. "You know, from *Easy Rider*. Everyone hip stays here. Jane Fonda. Jimmy Page. Bob Dylan. The place is crawling with famous people. Why do you think we're here?"

I thought we were hiding. So I sat in the lobby with the ship's log and peered up at everyone exotic who walked through the front door. Then, quickly, I tried to write a few lines describing them. Nobody looked famous. They all looked tired and strung out. The common difference between the men and the women is the women had fresh lipstick—their one attempt at sanitary glamour. Otherwise their clothes, especially their tights, platform shoes, and ratty hairstyles were as frenzied as they were filthy. They had plenty of style, but did nothing all day but cat around.

I had done a lot of nothing lately. And I was itching to get paid and move on. I knew a few writers had lived at the

Chelsea. I asked the desk clerk and he had given me a list of names of authors who had either visited or written entire books there: Mark Twain, O. Henry, Theodore Dreiser, Thomas Wolfe, William Burroughs, Allen Ginsberg, Nelson Algren, and Arthur C. Clarke. It was pretty impressive. I went down to the Strand bookstore and bought books by the Chelsea authors. *Naked Lunch* by Burroughs and *Look Homeward, Angel* by Wolfe were a good start. And once again I began to think about what I would do with myself after I got my money. I knew I wanted to write books, but I wasn't sure how to get started. I did know that I wasn't going to get anything done by smoking hash and sitting in the lobby of the Chelsea, no matter how cool it was to do so.

By the second week we had sold most of the hash and the operation was winding down. We had made deliveries all over Manhattan, and I had started to relax. I told myself if there were cops they would have picked us up by now. I was constantly surprised by who bought from us: a burned-out hippie, a well-dressed woman, a dull guy you'd never look twice at, a man in a fake wig and mustache, a preppie college kid. We met them in apartments, parking lots, coffee shops, high-rise lobbies, and on street corners. Each delivery was fifty pounds or more, so a lot of money was changing hands. After each score Rik put the cash in a bank safe deposit box, and finally, after my constant begging, I was paid. Hamilton gave me a shoe box of ten thousand dollars in ten dollar bills. I loved my stash. I counted it. I rubbed my face in it. It smelled sweet and dirty. I played with it like a kid with a toy. I straightened up all the bills so they were facing the same way. I bought rubber bands and wrapped each hundred and thousand. It was glorious. I grinned from ear to ear. It was while I was seduced by the big pile of cash that Hamilton chose to ask if I wanted to sail the *Beaver* to England, where we would take a rest before heading out to wherever we could pick up another ton. He was eager to repeat the operation. The hitch was we couldn't buy from the same supplier because, as Rik revealed, they had paid the Moroccans in counterfeit American cash and didn't want to risk dealing with them again. "They're probably pissed," Hamilton added, smiling at how clever he had been. I bet they'd give him a matching smile with a knife right across his throat if they ever caught him.

He promised me a better cut of the deal. I had mixed feelings. Sure, I wanted more money, but I didn't look forward to spending six months on a boat with Hamilton. And no matter how hard I tried I still had a nagging feeling we were being watched. I told him I'd give it some thought, but I knew I was ready to take off. I wanted to get started on my future. I called a few colleges in New York and asked about writing programs. New York University had one, as did Hunter and Columbia. They all wanted to know if I'd come in for an interview. I hesitated. I wanted to go. But I just felt so weird. Here I was, hiding out at the Chelsea Hotel and wheeling a stolen shopping cart full of smuggled hash all over town. I just wanted to finish up the operation and clean up my act before arriving in person.

I told the colleges I'd call them back. They wanted to send me information. But I didn't have an address.

And then the shit hit the fan.

It was a Friday when it all went to pieces very quickly. We had sold almost all the hash. There were only a few hundred pounds remaining. Hamilton and I were in our room when Rik called. He had another delivery to request, one that would empty the boat. Hamilton wrote down the address and smiled broadly. He looked in the mirror and patted his beard into shape. "You stay here," he said. "Afterward Rik and I have to prepare the cash for shipment. I don't want to sail it over. We'll meet you back here for dinner."

"Okay," I said, and he left the room.

I had bought more film and wanted to take photos of the room doors where the writers had lived. I knew Thomas Wolfe had lived in room 831. I had recently finished *Naked Lunch* and wanted to see where Burroughs had been insane, or brilliant, or both. I figured I'd go down and ask the desk clerk if he could give me Burroughs's room number.

I was on the second floor landing when I heard a scuffle downstairs by the front desk.

"We're FBI!" shouted a man. "Stop it." There was the fleshy slap of punches being thrown and Hamilton cursing. There were more punches and I heard Hamilton cry out, "Okay, okay, don't hurt me. Don't!" They must have had him pinned down.

I was frozen on the landing, unable to move. I couldn't see the front desk from where I was and I didn't dare look around the corner to see exactly what was happening. But I did want to hear if he was going to rat me out, or if they knew I was there. I could see the front door and watched the usual lobby druggies who crashed out across the furniture all day hop up and slink out the front door. As they did so, two scruffy men walked in.

Suddenly Hamilton shouted, "There they are! Those are the guys who own the boat."

It was a stroke of genius. The FBI agents let him go for a moment as they ran toward the men he'd fingered. At that moment the scruffy men pulled out their own badges and hollered, "Treasury agents! Stop!" They had been tracking down the source of the American counterfeit money that showed up in Morocco, and by coincidence arrived at the Chelsea just seconds after the FBI. It took the four of them a moment to check badges, but by then Hamilton had snaked down the back hall and out into the alley. The Feds sounded like a horse posse giving chase.

My heart almost burst. I scampered back up the stairs. I ran down to the room, unlocked the door, closed it, and locked it from the inside. I grabbed my green duffel bag out of the closet. I opened it and checked on the cash and five kilos of hash I had taken as a tip. I opened my dresser drawer and threw in my clean clothes. I hoisted my bag up over my shoulder and went to the back window. I was entirely in a panic. There was a fire escape from my window that connected down to the alley. But Hamilton had run that way and I figured the police would be milling around out there. My best way out would be through the front door. It was either that or wait for them to come get me. I couldn't wait even if I wanted to. I was too frantic.

I opened my door, scanned the hall, clutched my bag, took a deep breath, and walked down the steps, through the lobby and out the front door. The entire time I felt an invisible hand about to grab my shoulder. My neck was clenched as hard as a tree stump. I was planning to flag a cab but the traffic was backed up so I just kept walking. I lowered my head, dodging people, passing people, growling, pushing between them to get farther and farther away. I made it down to 14th Street and into the first subway station I came to. I had a token. I decided

I would go back uptown, to Penn Station. I bolted through the turnstile and took the first train that arrived. I hopped on, but couldn't stand still. I pushed my way from car to car, until I couldn't go any farther. When I reached the front I turned around, duffel bag on my shoulder, and waited to spot the eyes that were searching for me. At least I'd see them coming. But not yet—nobody was on my trail. We pulled into a station and I hopped off and looked at a map. I ran down a hall to another platform and took another train, then another, until I got to Penn Station. I ran to the Amtrak terminal and checked the departure board. I could go to Boston or Florida. I figured I knew Florida better. I could go hide out at Davy's place at the motel until I figured out what to do.

The train didn't leave for an hour, so I went downstairs and found a movie theater. *A New Leaf* was playing. I bought a ticket and felt like Lee Harvey Oswald hiding out. Walter Matthau and Elaine May were talking to each other, but I couldn't follow them. I sat there with my heart beating and sweat pouring out of me. I kept checking my watch. Finally it was time, and I dashed out of the theater, up the stairs, and across the terminal to the platform, where I hopped on the train and found a seat. Minutes went by, then the train began to move, and for a moment I thought, I've made it. I've escaped. I felt a little clever, but my heart didn't stop beating quickly until I went to the bathroom and swallowed a couple grams of hash and later fell asleep in my seat and woke up in North Carolina. Even then I was still a wreck.

When I got to Fort Lauderdale I stumbled off and called Davy's. She had a room available. I took a cab to the King's Court. I was so happy to be there, and Davy was happy to see me.

"Welcome back to the Alamo," she hollered when I opened her door. "What are you doing in town?"

"Just passing through," I said. "I sailed a boat up to New York and am on my way back to St. Croix."

"Well, stay as long as you want," she said, and gave me the key to my old room. "You'll see half of your friends are still here."

I walked across the asphalt, opened the door, and put my bag down. I double locked the door and pulled the curtains. I had made it. But I felt worse, and was worse off, than when I had first entered this room less than a year before. I sat down on the edge of my bed and held my face in my hands.

I jumped up. I went into the yellow bathroom and took off my clothes. I turned on the shower. As I waited for the water to warm up I stared into the mirror at my face. The yellow still wasn't a color that looked good on me. But it was home. I figured I'd take a shower, settle down, and plan out what to do next.

1 / evidence

My Lawyer's name, no kidding, was Al E. Newman, and the entire time I spoke to him over the telephone I thought I was talking to the grinning freckle-faced Alfred E. Newman on the cover of *Mad* magazine. It was unsettling.

My dad found him for me. The day after I checked in with Davy I walked down to a pizza parlor and called Dad from a pay phone.

He picked up.

"Hi," I said, "it's me."

"Where the hell are you?" he shouted back. Before I could answer he went into a harangue. "For Christ's sake, the FBI has been all over my ass. The phone has been tapped—they're probably listening to this now—they open our mail, they watch the house, they follow us around like we're criminals and keep asking if we've heard from you. What the hell have you done? Rob Fort Knox? They won't tell us—they just keep saying it was awful, which has nearly killed your mother. So, where the hell are you?"

"A pizza parlor," I replied, pretty much stunned after his monologue topped off my last two days. I had been hoping that, if they caught Hamilton or not, I had gotten away without a trace. But I was wrong. They knew who I was and they were searching for me, and I knew I was in trouble.

My father started back up. "I got in touch with a lawyer in New York," he said. "That's where you'll go to court, he claims."

"You already spoke with him?"

"Yeah. I know his brother from down here. Now, get with it, son. You are screwed to the wall. Call the lawyer and get some advice before they throw a net over you. It's always better to turn yourself in. Believe me, I've known enough criminals in my life."

"Okay," I said. "Okay."

"Well, do it," he persisted. "Besides, your mother is suffering overtime. God only knows why she loves an ingrate like you, but she does."

"How are things going with the business?" I asked, hoping to gain some relief with a change of subject.

"Jesus," he cursed. "The island is sinking under the waves. Houses are broken into every night. People are being shot. The only good thing about having a screw-up for a son is that the FBI is watching the house day and night, so I can sleep like a baby. Now, pay attention to your own business and call the lawyer." He gave me his name and number. "And keep me informed day by day," he said, before hanging up.

I called Al E. Newman.

"Yeah, I spoke with your father," he said. "And I already called the district attorney. They want to meet with you. I set up an appointment for tomorrow afternoon to turn yourself in. Where are you?"

I told him.

"Well, get yourself up here pronto," he advised. "In a case where there are a lot of guys involved you don't want to be the last guy to turn yourself in. It's like that game—musical chairs—last one down is a loser."

"Do I have to turn myself in?" I asked.

"No," he said in a deadpan voice. "You can hide out until they catch you, and they will. And they'll be totally pissed off and throw the book at you, which according to the prosecuting attorney is seventy-five years. Do you know you made the newspaper? Nice work."

I grinned like an idiot. There I was, wanted by the FBI. I should have been pulling my hair out. Instead, I was basking in my criminal glory. "I'll be up as soon as I can," I said. "Tell them I'll turn myself in."

After I got off the phone I went back to the motel and checked out. Davy was disappointed.

"Are you in trouble?" she asked.

"I think so," I replied.

"Well, don't go down without a fight," she advised. "That's what Davy always said."

They may have been his last words, I thought.

I caught a taxi to the main branch of the Fort Lauderdale library. The taxi waited as I ran into the newspaper reading room and found the paper Newman mentioned. On the front page there was a photograph of the *Beaver* with the story. The picture was taken at the 79th Street Marina. They had Hamilton sitting on some gear, squatting with his face hidden between his knees. It was a sad shot. I ripped the story out of the paper, folded it into my pocket, and ran back to the taxi. "Fort Lauderdale airport," I said.

On the way, I read the article. Some facts were mixed up but the important stuff was true: Two men had sailed a boat from Morocco to New York with two thousand pounds of hashish. One man was captured. One was still "an unknown suspect."

That was old news. The Feds already had my name. I caught a flight to New York, and once I landed I caught a taxi to the Chelsea Hotel. I was right back to where I'd started, but it was the only place I knew and since I was going to turn myself in it didn't seem dangerous anymore. I had read enough crime novels to know the *real* criminal runs. Only an idiot would return to the scene of the crime.

When I checked in I asked the clerk for room 273, our old room. It was available. I lugged my duffel bag up the stairs and unlocked the door. It looked pretty much just as I had left it. I opened a dresser drawer. Hamilton's stuff was still there. His T-shirts, underwear, and shorts. I pulled them out. Beneath them were his boating knife and a hash pipe. Remarkable, I thought. I opened another drawer. My books were where I'd left them. But the ship's log was missing. Had I taken it with me? Had I lost it somewhere? I couldn't remember.

I opened the closet. Hamilton's denim jacket was still on a hook. A pair of his scuffed-up boat shoes was on the floor. It looked like nobody had even bothered to clear out the room.

I wondered if Hamilton had hidden anything, like money or hash. I lifted the mattress. There was nothing. I pulled out all the dresser drawers. I lifted the false ceiling tiles in the bathroom. I checked the curtain hems, the chair upholstery, inside the phone—everywhere. But there were no hidden treasures. Just spooky evidence of our having been there before. When I finally convinced myself there was no money hidden in the room, I took Hamilton's hash pipe and smoked a bowl and fell asleep. I was exhausted.

In the morning I went shopping at a discount store and bought a cheap navy blue suit off the rack. I picked out two matching shirts and a tie, some socks and dressy half boots. On my way back to the Chelsea I stopped and got a decent haircut. Later, after a hot shower and with the suit on, I looked like an Ivy League kid from the 1950s. It was a relief not to recognize myself.

Al E. Newman's office was on 21st Street, not far from the Chelsea Hotel. I walked over and rang the bell on his red brick townhouse.

"Come in," he said, smiling, and shook my hand. He was tall, muscular, and fit—nothing like his *Mad* magazine counterpart. He held the door and as I passed by him he smelled clean, like the inside of a bar of soap. I thought that maybe, just maybe, he could clean up after me now.

He directed me to a wood-paneled office with walls lined with law books, school diplomas, and family photographs. He sat behind his busy desk and cut right to the point.

"I spoke with the prosecuting attorney, Mr. Tepper," he said. "We'll see him in an hour. But first, let me get you up to date. We're going to keep this an all-federal offense. No state involvement, which is good, because the state prisons stink. Always remember, if you have to do time, you want to be in a federal pen—so plan your crimes accordingly."

I didn't realize people gave their criminal activities so much advance thought.

"So, I asked Tepper," he continued, "what the indictment looked like and he said they have you listed for fifteen five-year charges. Twelve of the charges are for conspiracy to distribute a controlled substance, one for conspiracy to smuggle, one for conspiracy to possess counterfeit currency, and one charge of conspiracy to possess."

"Everything is *conspiracy*," I said. "What proof do they have?"

"He won't say over the phone," Mr. Newman replied. "We'll soon find out and plan our defense based on the strengths and weaknesses of their evidence. I'm hoping to build a case around the idea that you were just hired to sail the boat and didn't know anything about the hash. Let's start with that premise and see what he has to shoot it down."

"Okay," I said. I had no other choice, but I figured it was unlikely that premise would hold up.

We walked outside and caught a taxi to the Foley Square courthouse. Tepper's office was upstairs. "You gonna be okay?" Newman asked.

"I'm scared," I said honestly.

"Well, suck it up," he advised. "This is hardball."

After we all shook hands in Tepper's office he smiled smugly and said, "This is the most airtight case I've ever taken before a judge."

"All your charges are conspiracy based," Newman replied. "You don't have a case."

"Then take a look at this," Tepper said. He smiled a kind of "checkmate" smile and flipped open a manila folder that was about an inch thick with documents. "First, you are the last one to come out of the woodwork, which means everyone in front of you has *snitched* your *ass* out. We caught everyone you sold to, and every one of those dealers has named you as a person they bought from. And take a look at this." He flipped the page and there was Rik's mug shot taken in Miami. He had gone there from St. Croix before going up to New York. "We busted this yo-yo for shipping twenty-seven pounds of hash in a crate—and turned him like a key. He unlocked the whole operation. We had you followed all the way from St. Croix. Here are aerial photos of the boat taken from a Coast Guard surveillance plane."

Rik was the snitch. And suddenly on another photograph, there I was, the idiot waving to the turboprop that passed over us after that storm off Cape Hatteras.

"And look at this," he said, uncovering photographs taken by the Coast Guard launch in Cape May. "And this." He had photographs of the hash stashed in the boat—in the fo'c'sle and aft cabin, taken when they boarded the boat at the Flushing Marina. "Then we have photos of you at the boat loading hash into a shopping cart—look at the smile on your face. Would you like a mirror to see how you look now?" he asked sarcastically. He was enjoying himself and I could feel myself becoming more and more numb as I was beaten down. "And here are photos of you and Hamilton and Rik at the Chelsea, and let's see . . ." He shuffled through the papers. "We have a photo of you delivering to your buyer drop points, and finally, here's a mug shot of Hamilton after we popped him."

Poor Hamilton. There he was with his angry eyes and his beard roughed up, and all I could think of was him saying, *There is always a snitch.*

"I thought he got away," I said quietly.

"Almost," he replied, with a chuckle. "Get this. He runs out the back door of the Chelsea and down an alley. Somehow, we lose him. Can't find him anywhere—which is why we stopped paying attention to you for a bit—so Hamilton hops in a cab, but the traffic is all backed up because we started blocking the streets. He gets out and runs to a barbershop to get his big beard cut off. But the barber says, 'Oh no, it is too beautiful to cut.' And he refuses, so Hamilton runs out to find another barbershop and we pop him. Ha."

I looked at Newman. He had a game face on. I had no game face. I had no game, and I knew it. Newman knew it. And Tepper certainly knew it.

"Still," Newman said, trying, "you don't have my client in the act."

"Give me a break," Tepper replied. "This case is a lock. I have a statement by everyone popped that Gantos was part of the operation. Not to mention that Rik—who hired him—is set to testify."

"So what are you offering?" Newman asked.

"Gantos here gives us the names of all his St. Croix contacts and we'll tell the judge he cooperated."

Newman gave me an expectant look. I didn't know anyone on St. Croix who sold dope. I never even bought any when I was there. Rik gave me enough hash to keep me high until we dug up the stash.

"I don't know anyone who sells," I said.

"Well," he said, and closed the folder. "You think about it, because your only value to us is who you can rat out." He glanced at his watch. It was nearly 6 p.m. "I need a drink," he announced.

I did, too.

At a little bar around the corner Newman told me to buck up. "Every dog has his day," he said. "We let him have his. I'll call him tomorrow and see what we can plead to. Despite the fact that he's a real S.O.B.—he does have a seamless case against you."

"That's for sure," I said. At that moment I didn't feel so guilty as stupid. Really stupid. So stupid I could hear Mr. Bacon's voice predicting I would fall flat on my ass. I had, and I was angry. And I was angry that Rik had ratted us out right from the beginning.

That night I went out and bought Chinese food and a collection of Poe stories. I was reaching for anything to escape into, even "The Pit and the Pendulum."

Newman called the next afternoon and woke me up. "Okay," he announced, "here's the deal. We plead guilty to one charge of conspiracy to distribute and they drop the rest. They want to make it simple."

"What do you think?"

"You do it," he replied without hesitation. "Besides, there's a good chance you'll just get five years' probation."

"When do we plead?"

"We can file the plea now, and go for sentencing on the 22nd."

"What do you think will happen?" I asked. "Seriously."

He paused. "Don't sweat it," he replied. "You're just a kid."

2 / face-to-face

Every day, for the three weeks I stayed at the Chelsea Hotel while waiting for my sentencing, I worked over my face in the mirror. I just couldn't believe how ugly I was becoming. At first I was horrified. It was as if I had contracted a disfiguring disease that was slowly but surely reshaping my face. Huge lumps heaved up under the skin. Blemishes surfaced. Brown marks appeared as if I were rotting fruit. I knew I shouldn't touch my skin with my fingers, but I couldn't help it. I discovered pools of oil and pus under my skin. They drove me into a frenzy. I went right at them. I squeezed down on the welts with my fingers while pressing up against them with my tongue. They exploded, and coils of yellow matter and blood streamed down my face. I squeezed until the cavities were drained. This was very satisfying, this cleansing ritual. I'd punish my face as if I were a cop roughing up a suspect for a confession. Then, after an intense session, I'd step out of the bathroom and pace the carpet while smoking my hash pipe.

I figured my face was the landscape of my attitude. Each

day I woke and asked myself what I should do to avoid the possibility of going to prison. I could go to Canada. But then I'd have to spend the rest of my life there. That seemed unlikely. I could alter my identity, but I didn't know how to change my face, or my fingerprints, or even how to get a fresh set of ID's. The only thing I could change was my attitude, and that was changing for the worst. My only sensible plan was to sit tight, go to court, and hope for probation.

After Tepper had revealed all the government's super sleuthing, I figured they were still spying on me. And they were. In my room I kept the curtains pulled, the door locked, and the television turned up loud. I didn't like using my room phone except for ordering food. I'm sure it was bugged. And during the day there was always an agent camped out in the lobby, waiting for me, creeping up on me even as I called home from the pay phone by the back door steps. In the evening it was a different man. They followed me everywhere; if by accident or intent I lost them, we always met up again at the hotel. If I went to a restaurant, the agent stood outside. If I went to a bar, he came in. One night I read Dylan Thomas at the White Horse Tavern, the poet's favorite bar, and drank too much. On the way back to the hotel I staggered into an alley and began to vomit. At the end of the alley, leaning against a wall, the agent stood and watched me. "Leave me alone!" I spit out. He lit a cigarette and didn't say a word. I was trying to kill myself and they were letting me have a go at it.

The next day I worked my face over so heavily it looked like I had been punched around. I didn't care. The only relief I had was the few moments each day when I could pinch and squeeze and knead the reservoirs of blood and pus from under my skin.

It didn't take long to learn how to shake the agents. I'd just get on the subway and dash from train to train a dozen or so times, and before long I'd lose them. I did this after I had set up interviews at Hunter College and New York University. Both schools had writing programs, and both asked me for writing samples to accompany an application. I lied to them. I filled out the applications and promised I'd mail the sample in. But I knew I wouldn't. I had never written anything that was finished. I felt like a fraud. I returned to my room and worked over my face. I didn't have a typewriter. I didn't have ideas. But I had my face. And when I finished punishing it, I settled down for a while and went for a walk to think about what I might write for a sample. But it didn't take me long to find a bar, and for my agent to find me.

I spent a lot of money on drinks and meals while reading books. I read as much jail literature as I could locate. *On the Yard, Papillon, The Thief's Journal, Seven Long Times.* It was all depressing, but it was a distraction from obsessively picking at my face. When I couldn't find jail books, I read concentration camp books and P.O.W. books. I read *This Way to the Gas, Ladies and Gentlemen* four times in three weeks. I was living off the voices of other people's pain. Those writers had been worse off than I was now, and still they survived to write about it. I knew my fear was as real as theirs, but my words were still submerged. It was easier to pick at the scabs on my face than put pen to paper. Like those other writers, I figured I'd have to wait until the pain subsided and left the words behind.

One morning, for something to do, I lost my agent in the subway system and went to Lucas's apartment. We had sold him a hundred pounds of hash. He was a nice guy, and his apartment was filled with books, so I figured he was interesting, too. I knew he had been arrested and I was desperate to talk to someone who shared my messed-up feelings and situation. I thought he might be sympathetic. But Lucas wasn't home. His wife answered the door and invited me in. She informed me that he was in West Street—the federal detention center downtown. After his arrest she didn't want to bail him out. This was his second bust. They had two kids. She was pissed at him, and pissed at me.

"You'll both be sentenced on the same day," she said harshly. "He expects to do time. And if I were you, I'd expect it, too. That prosecuting attorney, Tepper, is a rabid dog and he's going to take a bite out of you."

"I know," I mumbled, and I was filled with dread. Still, I didn't care how blunt she was. It was just good to talk to another person even if she was using me to get a load off her chest. But a baby began to cry and she asked me to leave. At the door she had a few final words.

"You like to sell it, but did you ever consider what it could do to the people who bought it?"

I didn't know what to say right off, and she wasn't waiting.

"Figures you'd be struck dumb with that one," she said acidly, then slammed the door. I stood there for a minute. A minute was all I could endure because I was beginning to feel how I had screwed up more lives than just my own.

I went down to the corner and called Mr. Newman. I told him about Lucas expecting time. He probably knew this already, but I suddenly had the urge to keep talking.

"Don't worry," he said. "He's older, and he's a two-time loser. You're a kid. They won't do much to you. I'm betting on probation. You'll get off, and then move on with the rest of your life."

"Thanks," I said. But I had a hollow feeling inside. Somehow I knew this would never be over.

One morning I took a long walk uptown to the 79th Street Marina on the Hudson. I wanted to see the boat, but it was gone.

"Impounded," the dock manager told me when I asked. "The police have a place where they hold them and then auction them off."

I sat down on the dock. The river smelled like something dead. The sky was gray. I sat there and cried. I felt sad, and I hated myself for it. I felt beaten, and I hated myself for that. I didn't have one friend. I couldn't write one word. I was just waiting for the one day to arrive when my entire life would pivot. And I was sure things were not going to pivot my way.

Then the waiting game got worse. It was September 13th. I was watching the news. I had been following the Attica Prison uprising. Tom Wicker and William Kunstler had been reporting on the awful prison conditions at the big New York state pen. The place was horrifying. The guards were frightening. The prisoners were even more frightening. One guard had been killed in the uprising, and thirty-nine more were taken hostage. The prisoners had taken over the prison and were asking for amnesty. Wicker and Kunstler were helping to negotiate. But Governor Rockefeller was tired of talking and called in the troops. He had them ring the prison walls and fire down into the yard. Four thousand shots were fired in ten minutes. Twenty-nine prisoners were shot dead. The troopers also shot ten guards in the process. I sat there numbly watching the naked prisoners with their hands on their heads being lined up in the yard, poked with rifles, and shoved around by troops who behaved like Nazis. I knew bad things were going to happen to me. Guards weren't going to protect me. Prisoners weren't going to protect me. I was screwed. I stood up and went into the bathroom and savagely worked my face over.

The days passed. My fear grew. My face remained an open wound. The night before my sentencing I wrapped my remaining hash, about two pounds, in plastic bags. I shoved it down my pants, turned out all the room lights, and opened the back window. I stepped onto the fire escape and worked my way down to the alley. A few blocks later I flagged a taxi and went uptown, to 50th Street. I went into a little variety store and bought a metal serving spoon. I had to bury the hash and I figured Central Park was the best place. I walked several blocks to the park entrance across the street from the Plaza. I was scared. I kept thinking someone was watching me. I kept looking around for any of the agents, and also for a place to dig a hole, a place that wouldn't be bothered if I had to do time. As I walked I heard the clomping horses pulling buggies on the street. Finally I looked around and saw a stone drinking fountain. I stood next to it. From there I could see the statue of General Sherman on his horse.

"Okay," I said to myself. "Remember this spot and then this map." I took thirty-nine steps to the west because I liked the movie *The Thirty-nine Steps*. Then I took twenty steps to the north, one for each year of my life. That brought me into some bushes. "Take *Fifteen Steps to Better Writing* to the west then turn around and dig," I whispered. I tramped fifteen paces through the underbrush. I squatted down and cleared the ground with my hands. Then I began to dig. The ground was filled with rocks and roots. It was slow going, and I couldn't see much of what I was doing. I just kept stabbing at the hole with the spoon, then clawing at the roots and rocks with my hands until I could get them out of the way and then stab at the ground some more.

It took forever. Probably an hour. When I finally shoved the hash down all the way I bent the spoon in half and left it in the hole. I filled it up with the rocks and dirt and stomped the mound down, then gathered leaves and spread them over the dirt. Then I began to march away. "Fifteen, twenty, thirty-nine," I counted out, until I was back at the water fountain. I looked over to salute General Sherman and walked toward the park exit.

In the morning I woke up early and packed all my belongings into a bunch of cheap nylon bags I had bought from a street vendor a few days before. I took a scalding hot shower, worked over my face for the last time, and got dressed in my cheap suit. I was ready.

I checked my bags with the front desk at the hotel. I paid

for my bill in cash. "Either I'll pick my bags up later today, or I'll send someone around to do so," I said.

The receptionist shrugged. He couldn't care less.

I looked into the lobby. There were two agents. It was sentencing day, and they didn't want to lose me.

3 / a long, long day

I met Mr. Newman at Foley Square. I had one thing on my mind. Probation. I didn't want to do time. Hamilton was right. I wasn't afraid because I thought smuggling hash was wrong—I was afraid because of the punishment.

"Your dad called my office," Newman said. "He's going to be late but he'll meet us in the courtroom. He'll be there to make a statement if we need him."

I looked around the square. I didn't see him. The agents stood a long ways off. I handed Mr. Newman an envelope with the last of my money—$5,700 in cash. I had gone to a bank and changed the ten dollar bills into hundreds. "Take your fee out of this and keep the rest for me in case I go away," I said.

He nodded, and slipped it into his jacket pocket. Then he looked at his watch. "You ready?" he asked.

We went up to the courtroom. We were the first case on the docket. The judge arrived and we stood.

The judge sat down and opened the top file on his desk. He read a page or so, then peered out toward us. "Does the prosecution have anything to add to the pre-sentencing report?" he asked Tepper.

"Your Honor," Tepper started, and he went on to once again give an outline of the operation. He revealed all the evidence proving my involvement, and outlined what laws I broke. Then he went a little further. "The accused has not cooperated in the ongoing investigation of others involved with this international operation. It is our belief that he is withholding information, and our office is in favor of incarceration."

"I see," the judge replied, and adjusted his glasses as he wrote something down. "And you, Mr. Newman, what do you have to say on behalf of your client?"

I looked at Newman. We had been hurt pretty badly by Tepper and I was waiting for him to battle back.

"Your Honor," he said, "Mr. Gantos fell into this situation. He was hired merely to help sail the vessel to New York. He did not belong to an international operation, or in any way plan this failed smuggling trip. Mr. Gantos is a young man who has made a grown man's mistake. But unlike a grown man he has a full life ahead of him. He regrets his actions. He willingly admits that probation and a drug treatment program would be in his best interest. He has plans for college and a life free of future violations. Prison can only punish a young man with his background and future. We are asking for your consideration regarding his age and—"

The judge had heard it all before. He was immune to the nice-young-man defense. He raised his hand and cut Mr. Newman off. "And, young man," he said loudly, "what might you say for yourself?"

I stood there. Frozen. Now it was my turn. I looked at Mr. Newman. I turned to see if my father had arrived. He hadn't. I looked at Tepper and back at the judge. "I made a mistake," I said. "A big mistake."

I guess I didn't sound sorry enough, or speak quickly enough.

"A criminal mistake? Or just the mistake of getting caught?" the judge roared back.

And then I just stopped functioning. I stood there knowing the truth was that I was sorry I was caught, and if I hadn't been I would just have moved on to college and this would be a great story I could tell my friends after drinks and a joint.

"Well?" the judge asked. "Which is it? Bad judgment? Or bad luck?"

I hesitated. Maybe for only a second. But it was a second filled with a lifetime like it is for the condemned Southerner in *An Occurrence at Owl Creek Bridge*, whose life passes before his eyes from the moment the hangman pulls the lever until the rope snaps his neck. And while I was stuck within that endless moment, I was doomed. Tepper stepped forward and finished me off.

"Your Honor," he began. "May I read to you something that Mr. Gantos wrote while on the ship?"

When I saw him holding the ship's log the shock of it pulled me out of myself. That's where it went! They must have found it when they searched the room. I knew what he was up to. He had the pages marked with ribbons as if it were a Bible marked for readings.

"Proceed," the judge said.

"I believe this one section says it all about how Mr. Gantos feels. And I read from the ship's log: *Hamilton had read my mind—I'm not doing anything wrong. I'm just afraid of the punishment.*" He snapped the book closed, looked over at me, and smiled.

"Did you write those words?" the judge asked.

"Yes, sir," I replied.

"Then I believe we have gotten down to the truth of the matter," he said. "And the truth is always in the motivation. You did it for the money. That much is true. Now the law must respond." He paused, and in that moment I stood there as if my hands were already tied behind my back, waiting for the first blow of many. And it came.

"5010B," the judge called out matter-of-factly. He lowered his gavel and a split second later bellowed, "Next!"

I turned to Mr. Newman. "What's a 5010B?" I asked.

"I don't know," he said, puzzled. "I'll have to look it up."

"So, what do I do?" I looked around. Everyone seemed to be standing still except for a uniformed court guard who was reaching toward me.

"You'll have to go with him," Mr. Newman said somberly, and nodded toward the guard who had taken hold of my wrist. As he led me across the courtroom I passed in front of my father, who had just arrived. He looked stunned. For once he was speechless, and had I not been so entirely shocked and confused I might have paused long enough to realize the look on his face was from the anguish that his son was being marched off to federal prison. But I was overwhelmed by my own pain.

"I took a risk," I said, and bit down on my lip. "It didn't pan out."

I waited for him to say something and when he didn't, or couldn't, the guard tugged me forward and I turned away and followed. We went into an office and the guard patted me down, took my wallet and what change I had in my pocket, my watch and belt, then he locked me in a holding cell lined with wooden benches. I looked around. There were guys like me dressed in street clothes who had been out on bail and were now sentenced. And there were guys in prison clothes who hadn't made bail after their arrest and were now awaiting sentencing. One after the other the men in prison clothes were escorted into court, then returned to the cell. Not one of them was released. Each time one returned he announced how much time he had received. Three years, five years, twelve years. One armed bank robber got twenty years. He sat and cried. Even the shortest sentence, three years, was more than I could imagine. Slowly, from watching the pain well up in those men, I began to feel the consequences of what had happened to me.

A couple of hours later the guard opened the cell door and called me out. For a fleeting moment I thought maybe the judge had changed his mind, or that there had been an awful mistake and everyone now realized that I was really a good kid and now they were going to give me a slap on the wrist and let me go. But I was dreaming. The guard escorted me to a room where my lawyer was waiting.

"I finally spoke with the judge's clerk," he said. "Here's the situation. A 5010B is a youth sentence. It means you can do anywhere from sixty days to six years, depending on your behavior and what the parole board thinks."

"What do you think?" I asked. "Do you think I'll just do sixty days?" I felt I could do that much.

"I don't know," he replied, not sounding hopeful. "It will be up to the parole board. I'll look into it, but don't get your hopes up too high."

As he left the room, my dad entered.

"What will I tell your mom?" he asked, as he sat down.

I hung my head. "Tell her I made a huge mistake," I said. "Tell her I'll be okay. I'll be out soon. Tell her that."

While he thought about it the air between us filled with quiet confusion. It was unsettling. I would rather have been in the cell than sitting silently with him. At least by myself I only had my pain to consider. But his silence left me feeling his pain, and that of the entire family. And in front of him I was ashamed, too. Then as if by magic he did something that turned all my feelings around. All the pain knotted itself up into anger.

He pulled a set of folded papers out from inside his jacket pocket. "I almost forgot. I need you to sign something," he said, fishing around in his pants pocket for a pen.

"What's this?" I asked.

"Car insurance papers," he explained. "Your car is totaled and I need you to sign this release so the insurance company can pay me."

"What happened?" I asked. And suddenly I hated him, which was easier to do than feel the unrelenting weight of my shame. "What happened!"

"It went down the cliff," he said. "It's a good thing. Look, with everyone fleeing nobody would buy that car. An accident is the only way you can get some money for it."

"How'd it happen?" I asked.

"Your sister was driving and knocked a hole in the oil pan

and the engine seized up when she was climbing the hill. So I got the pickup and drove down and gave your car a shove off the edge. She drove the pickup home, and I kind of rolled down the hill a bit and got myself dirty to make it look like I had been run off the road and managed to bail out. The car was pretty amazing. It bounced down the hill on all fours until it hit the lower road. The damn thing bent in half and skidded across the road into someone's yard and wouldn't you know it, they were having a barbecue." He grinned and shook his head back and forth. "You should have seen them scatter as that car came through their front yard," he said with a laugh. "Lordy, it was funny."

"That's my insurance money," I said.

"I need it to pay my air fare," he replied. "Business is bad. Plus our lives have been hell. We've all been followed around by the cops. They searched the warehouse. They were even up in the yard looking for plants. I don't think you realize what has been happening to us, so the car money will help."

He had me there. I hadn't realized what had been happening to them. I had been entirely involved with myself. I signed the papers. "Sorry," I said, as I pushed them back to him. "I'm sorry about all of this. Tell Newman to give you a thousand dollars, but now it's time for me to get on with it."

He looked at me. "I should have known that Rik guy was no good. I never should have let you get on that boat. I blame myself. I just thought it was your ticket out of the mess down there—I didn't see that it would lead to all this." He motioned to the walls and bars.

"This is all my fault," I said. "Not yours."

I stood up and signaled with my hand for the guard. He opened the door. I turned and walked off. I didn't look back because no matter how disappointed I was with my car or my life, if I saw him crying I would, too, and I knew I couldn't cry because I had to enter a roomful of men who were watching me very closely. And I figured they were not looking for signs of friendship. They were looking for signs of weakness.

The first night was the worst. After waiting all afternoon at the Foley Square courthouse holding pen, we were handcuffed together and lined up in the hallway. There must have been two dozen of us. A guard led us down a long passage to a freight elevator. We all squeezed in. When the door opened we stepped out onto a loading dock. A black bus with open back doors backed up to the loading dock, and one by one our handcuffs were unlocked and we shuffled aboard, filling up the bus benches front to back. There were windows with bars and chicken wire in the glass panes. Nobody talked. There was a lot of sniffing. Not crying sniffing, but sniffing like dogs as if you could smell everyone's fear, everyone's sour sweat, the smell of our exhalation, the lunch, the bile, the illness in everyone all breathing out and filtered back in. Outside, New York only seemed to exhale—horns, voices, machines, tires, sirens, helicopters, music, protests, advertisements—all pushing out the air, all selling noise. But we weren't buying anymore. We weren't selling anymore. Now all our robbing and scamming and dealing and running would take place on the inside. Now we only had each other to deal with and we were all busy sniffing each other out and coming up with some sense of who was dangerous and who was not.

We pulled up to West Street. It was a federal holding prison built inside Dutch Schultz's old liquor warehouse, which had been confiscated during Prohibition after Dutch was arrested.

I got lucky. I was one of the last in the prison bus so I was one of the first ones off, and immediately directed to the AR-RIVAL office. There I gave up my street clothes and was given a set of old army fatigues with the insignias ripped off. We were allowed to keep our shoes, so I kept my Frye black boots. I was given a washcloth and towel, extra underwear and socks, and was assigned to D-10. It was a large, barred cage, like the elephant's cage at the zoo. There were eighteen military bunk beds inside for thirty-six men. Because I was the next new man assigned to the tank I had the choice of the two empty bunks. I choose the top bed in a corner under a blue fluorescent light. It seemed the safest. The other bunk was in the middle, on the bottom, where I knew it would be dark at night and without a corner to protect my back. Lucas got that bunk. He must have been sentenced in a different courtroom and he arrived after me. It was late when he checked in and I was already up on my bed like Quasimodo guarding Notre Dame.

Later that night a guy with a metal dinner fork reached up and grabbed my arm. I jerked my arm away and cocked my legs back to kick him. I had kept my boots on.

"It's cool," he whispered. "Are you funny?"

I wasn't feeling funny. "What do you mean?"

"You know, funny. Like do you do it with guys?"

Now I knew I wasn't funny. "No," I said. "No."

"But you're young," he said. "You can still learn. I can be your master."

"I don't need a master," I said.

"Believe me, you do," he said. "You can either be my booty-boy and I'll protect you, or all these other dudes will take turns making you a mama."

"Go away," I said. My fear was so great I couldn't endure another moment of the conversation.

"You'll see," he said. "You got a tax on your ass and you'll have to pay up."

He disappeared into the darkness and I stayed awake. The next morning I didn't go down to breakfast, which meant going down two flights of stairs to the cafeteria. I didn't think I'd ever leave the safety of my top bunk with bars to my back. But I was dying to get to the bathroom, so once the floor cleared out I jumped off my bunk, quickly walked to the bathroom, and took a leak at the toilet closest to the door. I had read enough prison literature and seen enough prison movies to know that the bathroom, especially the shower room with its combination dangers of steam and soap, was a place to avoid at all costs. I was wondering if I could take a bath with a paper cup of water and a sock.

Just then a guy walked into the bathroom and came toward me. I zipped up.

"Yo," he said, "best be checkin' up on your man." He pointed to a toilet stall.

I was stumped. "What man?" I asked. I was rapidly thinking that he was setting me up and inside the stall was a gang of guys waiting to collect their "tax."

"Thanks," I said, not knowing if I should give him a soul brother handshake like all the righteous brothers in *Shaft*. He helped me out by walking away.

I didn't know what to do. I looked around like a nervous squirrel. "Lucas," I whispered. I ducked down to see under the stall door. Lucas was curled up like a shrimp with a blanket.

I looked over my shoulder, then opened the door. "What happened?"

He closed his eyes and pulled back the blanket. He was

naked. His legs had been mauled as if a pit bull had caught him from behind. He had been raped, and when he finished telling me what had happened—how many guys got him after dark, how the first man held his throat and mouth, more got his legs and arms and then they flipped him over on his belly and started, and only stopped once everyone finished their turn—I didn't know what to say.

"I'm sorry," I muttered lamely, feeling the total emptiness of my response.

"Help me stand," he said, and reached out for my shoulder. "My wife is coming to visit today."

I gave him a hand. I didn't know how sympathetic his wife would be. And, honestly, I was eager to get away from him. I was beginning to fill up with fear and wanted to put some distance between us. It was the fear of being with a victim, and that I would be next in line. I had that terror people must have had during the war, when they denied they were Jews or Gypsies or homosexuals as the Nazis dragged off their families and friends. At that moment I hated myself as much as I feared being around Lucas.

It was just twenty-four hours since I had been sentenced and I knew I was in way over my head.

4 / my yellow cell

*I was soon shipped out of West Street and sent to the fed—*eral prison in Ashland, Kentucky. By dumb luck I ended up in a private hospital cell when I arrived at Ashland. The receiving physician's assistant, Mr. Bow, spotted lice in my hair. I must have picked them up while sitting in a transfer prison in Washington, Pennsylvania, on my way from New York. Once Mr. Bow spotted the lice, he escorted me to a delousing shower room in the hospital and I washed with a parasiticide that smelled like licorice. Afterward, I was dusted with DDT and given clean clothes and assigned to a sunny yellow cell to relax until the lice died. I couldn't relax.

The color of that yellow cell got to me. It was a bright, smiling yellow that buzzed like a summer day. There was no hiding from that color. Like me, that yellow room had its ups and downs as the day wore on. The slightest fluctuation in the weather outside my window, the smallest passing cloud, the changing position of the sun affected the mood of that room. And my mood shifted with it. I found myself crying, laughing, numb with depression, nervous and pacing, ambivalent, angry, and filled with self-loathing. Even when I slept I kept the pillow over my eyes to keep the yellow from seeping through my eyelids, just as I used to keep my hand over my eyes to keep out the light when napping on the deck of the *Beaver*.

It was a great cell, as far as cells at Ashland Federal Prison went—eight feet by ten feet with a solid iron door fitted with a twelve-inch-square safety glass peep window, and a horizontal slot on the bottom for passing food trays in and out. I had a single bunk, a bedside storage locker, a toilet, sink, polished nickel mirror, and metal chair. Each was bolted to the concrete floor. And it was all mine. When I was locked in at night I could sleep without expecting someone to sneak up to rape me, or hit me, or cut me. I could go to the bathroom in private. I could sit and think in private.

I also had a window to the outside. Every few minutes I hopped up from my bunk and looked out beyond the bars at the red brick administration wing, and just beyond it to the picnic grounds where family members visited and ate lunch with minimum-security prisoners and guards on break. There were trees, and flower beds, and pine tables covered with red-and-white-checked tablecloths. It was green and peaceful out the window, and a break from the unrelenting yellow of my cell, which was like having the unblinking eye of the sun blaz-

155

ing on me each day, reminding me that prison was not the dark place where I could hide from my past—and definitely not the place where I could hide from myself. Even at night there was no relief from that color. At sundown the naked bulb overhead came on and beneath it I'd slump into a drama of my own self-interrogation. There was nothing else to do but beat myself up. That first week I had no books. No writing paper and pencil. No radio. No one to speak with. No cigarettes. No alcohol. No drugs. Just me, sitting on the edge of my bunk, slowly grilling myself under that yellow light.

At first I pointed the finger at everyone else—my family, my friends, the gang of backstabbers that I worked with in the smuggling ring. I burned them all on a bonfire of blame. But that didn't give me any relief. Had someone else been responsible for what I had done, I suppose my blaming them would have satisfied me. But it didn't. So I threw myself on the fire and went up like gasoline. I smuggled the hash. I took the money. I hurt my family. No fire rages like guilt.

Six times a day, like every other prisoner, I was counted at my bed. Each morning before breakfast the guard in the front office clicked on the intercom system. From the loudspeaker on my floor I could hear his amplified breathing. Then he'd sniff. Finally he'd bellow, "COUNT!" And from loudspeakers in every hallway, every dormitory, every work facility, on the outside of the buildings, from atop the guard towers and tele-phone poles located throughout the grounds, I could hear the echo of that "COUNT!"

Next I could hear the hospital guard's leather shoes tap-ping across the polished linoleum floor. As he briskly walked by my peep window I stood next to my bed and yelled back, "IN!" And as he passed every other occupied hospital cell the man inside stood next to his bed and yelled, "IN!"

I was in. Counted in. After breakfast I was counted. Before dinner I was counted. After dinner. Before lights out. Then while I slept. And even then I turned that phrase over and over in my mind: "Count me in." Those were three words I'd take back if I could. They were my words to Rik and Hamilton. "Count me in." Now I was counted in my cell every day, and I was counted on to be there morning, noon, and night.

Without books, I began to read the walls. Like a blind man reading Braille, I traced my fingers over the graffiti scratched into the concrete blocks. I puzzled out names and words, dates and shapes, and imagined the lives of the men who lived there before me, just as I had done in my old ex-prison high school. The coincidence of that connection made me laugh, and I think it was the first good laugh I had behind bars. I never would have guessed that the visit from the prison alumni I laughed at in high school had been an omen of my future.

Then I found the best line scratched above the mirror:

WHAT WE HAVE HERE IS A FAILURE TO COMMUNICATE. That line from *Cool Hand Luke* said it all for me, whether I was talking to myself or to someone else. Some wit had carved it into the cinder block so that each time he looked in the mirror he reminded himself that the biggest failure in life is self-communication.

After my first few days the food service worker who had been delivering the special hospital meals took pity on me bouncing off my yellow walls like a cricket trapped in a box. He brought me some books, a pad of paper, envelopes, and a pencil.

"Do whatever you want with the books," he said. "They were left in the cafeteria. The paper is regulation for writing letters home. When you finish one, give it to a floor guard. Keep in mind they read it before sending it out, and whoever gets it won't miss the U.S. Dept. of Corrections stamped on the envelope. You'll have to sharpen the pencil with your teeth."

"Thanks," I said. I looked over the books. There was a Zane Grey cowboy novel. An autobiography by Christine Jorgensen, who was the first man to have a sex change. I thought that was odd. And *The Brothers Karamazov* by Dostoyevsky. I stacked them up on my locker and sat down on the bed with the pad and pencil.

The first thing I did was write the judge and ask him to reduce my sentence to time served. I told him I had lice, had fully realized my mistakes, and had been scared straight. I addressed the letter to my lawyer and asked him to forward it to the judge. It was a long shot to send a jailhouse appeal, but from where I was sitting I had nothing to play but long shots.

Dostoyevsky had spent some time in prison. He wrote about it in *House of the Dead*. And I guess knowing that only encouraged me to use *Karamazov* for my journal. I read the book first. Then I began to record my own lines between his lines. Naturally, his were better. But mine were mine, and it didn't take me long to find out I had plenty to write about.

I set the journal up differently than I had my others. On each page I started writing between the lines and then broke out and wrote all crazy around the margins and every which way I could find some space so that it was all jumbled up. I tossed in everything I saw and thought and felt during the day and wrapped it all up with book quotes and prison slang and bits of wild conversation, and anything I thought was interesting. I didn't keep up my old habit of writing down my ideas for novels because it seemed unnecessary. I felt as if all the fictional ideas I cooked up were nothing compared to what was going on around me in real life.

I was reading when three black guys from the Muslim Brotherhood knocked on my door. They were very well groomed. Their nails shone, their skin glowed, and the hair beneath their elaborately crocheted skullcaps looked drawn on with conté crayon.

"Excuse me, brother," one of them said from the other side of the glass.

I looked up from my bunk, then turned away.

"Excuse me," he said again, and rapped the glass with his knuckles. "We'd just like to make a brief offer toward improving race relations."

"I'm not in on race-related charges," I replied. "I don't have those problems."

"That's wonderful," he replied in an unctuous voice. "Because we have an offer for you."

"What?" I asked, even though I really didn't want to know.

"More than ever before, the races need to trust each other. And I want to offer you an opportunity to enter the circle of trust between the black man and the white man."

Trust was a touchy subject for me. At present I didn't have any in anyone, no matter what the issue.

"So here is our offer," he said. "Every Sunday is movie night up in the gym. During the movie the Muslim brothers all gather in the bathroom for a little prayer meeting. What we would like once you are released into population is for you to join us in a ceremony of trust. Come meet the brothers and then we want you to pull your pants down around your knees and bend over."

I didn't say anything. I could hardly believe I heard him correctly.

"It's all about trust," he said, reminding me again of the larger point. "You see, by not fucking you when you are at your most vulnerable, you will realize that you can trust us, and we will trust you because you took a chance on our behalf. So what do you say? When you enter population will you meet us in the bathroom? The meeting will only take a minute."

"I'm sorry," I said, trying hard to sound practical, "but I don't go to movies."

"This is a golden opportunity," he said. "We don't offer it to everyone. Only a select few whom we believe can handle this type of trust."

"Well, no thank you," I said. "It's a wonderful offer, but I have other plans."

"Well," he said, "when your schedule permits, just let us know and we'll make a date."

At that moment the loudspeaker was flipped on and the rotunda guard hollered "COUNT!" They turned, and marched off.

After the count was cleared I flipped open my journal and wrote down everything that had just happened. Nobody would believe it. I couldn't. That's why I had to write it down.

After a week the physician's assistant opened my cell. He was a big man, with a head as wide as his shoulders. It made him look like a smiling toad. I liked him. I liked anyone who didn't look mean or dangerous.

"Let's see if those lice have had enough DDT," he said. I stripped down and he checked me from top to bottom. Then he ran a fine comb through my hair. "We have to be careful. Once we get an epidemic of lice, or crabs, or scabies, it is near impossible to get rid of 'em."

"I guess so," I said, trying to keep up my end of the conversation.

"Yeah," he continued. "I think these lice are cooked and you're ready to be sent down to population."

I didn't want to go into population—not after what I had seen happen to Lucas in West Street, and what I imagined was waiting for me in Ashland.

"You know," I said, "I once did some volunteer work in a hospital. Do you need any workers?"

"Funny you should ask," he replied. "My X-ray tech only just flipped out and tried to climb over the fence." He looked out my window and pointed to the spot. "I mean that kid just snapped. Broad daylight he runs from the dormitory, out across the yard, and starts to climb. Of course, they spotted him right away. Told him to come down, but he wouldn't, so they had to jerk him down with something like a gaff hook and now he's locked in isolation with a couple of broken ribs."

"Sounds pretty rough," I said, as I got dressed.

"Would you like a job as the X-ray tech?" he asked. "You could live up here and be part of the hospital staff."

"That would suit me fine," I said.

And just like that I fell into the best job in the prison. I got to keep my private cell. The medical staff trained me to use the X-ray machine and develop the film, and from then on I was always the first one called to X-ray the men who were injured during the night—especially those who lived in the hundred-and-twenty-man dormitories, where once the lights were turned off you could stealthily roam from bunk to bunk and settle a score with anyone. And they did. Nightly, it seemed to me. I also learned how to stitch up wounds (I practiced on chicken parts), properly apply tourniquets, tweeze shattered glass out of gashes, wash out eyes that had been burned with bathroom cleansers, pop dislocated bones back into joints, and perform an assortment of other triage skills.

It was a good job, and it allowed me to see the results of all the rough action in the prison, without having to be directly involved. Still, I knew I had to keep my guard up.

5 / drug lust

After I settled into my daily routine, I got used to sleeping and waking up behind a locked door. But it took more time to get used to the seesaw intensity of the place. When life was funny in prison it was hysterically funny. And when it was scary it was menacing. The trick was to observe everything and every person without becoming the object of anyone's negative attention. The effort to become invisible, or to appear nonthreatening yet dangerous, was exhausting, which is why in prison almost everyone wanted drugs. Not books. Not journals. Not pens. Not anything that would make you more aware of your pain. They wanted drugs to smoke, drugs to snort, drugs to swallow, and drugs to shoot directly into their veins by any means possible. If you took enough you could forget which side of the fence you were on. You could jail your own fears and drift away with the clouds. Drugs were smuggled in by family members and spouses every Sunday. The altar boys collected them in the offering baskets and funneled them through the church office. Food service workers brought them in and sold them to the cafeteria crews, who in turn had friends or relatives mail them the payments. Drugs were hidden in tennis balls painted grass green and thrown over the double rows of twelve-foot fences and into the exercise yards. They were carried in by trustees on work-release who wore boots with hollowed-out soles and traveled into town and back. Construction workers who came in to build new dormitories were talked into making deals. Hallucinogens were mailed in on drug-laced stationery. Even a few crooked guards brought them in. You could get anything you wanted for a price—from cocaine and heroin to reefer and a full range of pills to take you up, or down.

I could always smell reefer while out on the yard, and every now and again I'd see someone nodding off in the cafeteria. About once a week we had some kind of pill overdose or drug-related emergency at the hospital—often involving homemade works. Once a man stumbled up to the clinic with a metal needle used to inflate basketballs shoved into the crook of his arm. He had taped the clear tube of a ballpoint pen to the threaded end of the needle, and on top of that he had fixed a tennis ball. He told me he cooked the dope, poured it into the pen tube, jammed the sharpened point of the needle into his arm, attached the tennis ball, and gave it a good squeeze. The air pressure was supposed to drive the dope down through the needle and into the vein. Only it didn't work out that way. He oversqueezed the tennis ball, the air rushed down the tube, through the needle and directly into his vein, and by the time I saw him he had a quivering ball of air trapped in a vein over his biceps. Fortunately he had a belt wrapped tightly around his upper arm cutting his circulation, or he would have been dead from an embolism. I was on duty and squeezed the air back down his vein toward the puncture in his elbow. It hissed and sprayed blood as it came out. I kneaded his arm over and over until I couldn't feel any bubbles.

"You ready?" I asked, hoping there wasn't a bubble left that might lodge in his brain. He nodded and I unsnapped the tourniquet.

He whimpered a quick prayer, then sat there still as a statue until he figured the danger had passed. Then he unrolled his sleeve and dashed off down the main corridor before any hospital guards saw him.

While I was in my hospital cell I stayed away from the drugs. I wanted to escape into them—especially Valium and Librium, which were little pleasure pillows that I knew would dissolve my massive stress, if only for an evening. They were always for sale, but I didn't dare cop. I was too afraid of being caught, and I figured getting out of prison was more important than getting high in prison.

Because the hospital cells were off limits to the general population, we had a number of traveling prisoners stay with us.

Mostly they were men from the Witness Protection Program who were in organized crime, had snitched, and were on their way somewhere else. They'd stay for a few days until U.S. Marshals arrived to take them to a secret destination.

We also warehoused all the men in on rape charges until they were sent to prisons with sexual offender programs. Guys in for rape were never put into general population. Prisoners didn't like the thought of being behind bars while their mothers, wives, girlfriends, or children were preyed upon. No rapist would have survived in population.

One day I woke up to find a different kind of visitor. He was an Elvis impersonator, and when I asked him his name he replied without hesitation, "Elvis Presley."

"Nice to meet you, Elvis," I said.

He was on tour, traveling from prison to prison to put on shows while working down a five-year sentence for mail fraud—selling fake Elvis memorabilia through magazines. I found him absolutely incredible. He looked like the young Elvis in rolled-up blue jeans and a denim shirt. His hair was dyed perfectly blue-black. He practiced singing while holding a guitar with no strings—a guitar string was considered a potential weapon for garroting people and he was only given his strings just before a concert, and then had to give them back. His a cappella voice was very true, though, and it was wonderful to hear him practice "Blue Suede Shoes," "Heartbreak

Hotel," and "In the Ghetto" as I went about the hospital or-
derly business of changing bandages, taking vital signs, and
filling out charts. He gave a concert in the gym. I never at-
tended because a fistfight broke out between hecklers and hill-
billies and I was busy in the X-ray room taking shots of broken
knuckles and metacarpals.

He was gone the next day.

We had one female employee in the hospital—she was the administrator's assistant. We all called her Miss Kentucky, as she
was shapely and rolled her hips when she walked. Because
there were a few cases of tuberculosis in the prison, everyone
had to get a periodic chest X-ray. I took all the guards' shots,
and the prisoners', but Dr. Sokel, the head of the prison hospital, took Miss Kentucky's. I had to develop all the X-rays,
about six hundred of them. When I developed hers I could just
make out the outline of her breasts. It was a very faint soft tis-
sue impression. It took me a week of long hours to develop all
the X-rays and when I finished I had sorted the prisoners'
shots in alphabetical order, and I did the same with the guards'
stack. I put Miss Kentucky on top of that stack because she
was the only woman. One night I left all the X-rays on a light
table in the examination room. Somehow, somebody stole her
X-ray. I guess it was the equivalent of a *Playboy* centerfold for
someone. I reported it to Mr. Bow and he informed the guards.

They were upset over it and there was a general lockdown and cell search for the shot. It was found in the cafeteria bathroom and returned to her file. She quit shortly afterward.

A guy from Baltimore came up to the X-ray room to see me. He wanted a laxative. I told him to wait in the regular triage line for a physician's assistant. I was busy screening the new admissions for venereal diseases. He didn't want a laxative, he admitted. He really wanted an X-ray. That was against the rules. I asked him why he wanted one. A week ago, he said, his wife visited and during the course of the visit she slipped him a dozen Vaseline coated balloons full of hash which he swallowed, and he hadn't gone to the toilet since then and was feeling sluggish.

"You gotta help me," he pleaded. "I can't go to the doctor or I'll get busted."

I had him come back in an hour, after I'd finished my work. I put him in front of the fluoroscope without his shirt. I didn't like using it because it leaked a lot of radiation. I wore a lead apron and flipped the switch. "Move your gut around like a hula dancer," I said. He did. I spotted the train of balloons in his lower intestines. They looked whole, but impossible to tell for certain.

"You need an enema," I said.

"How do I get that?"

"Go down to the cafeteria and lift one of the ketchup squeeze bottles with the pointy top. Clean it out good and fill it with hot water and do what has to be done." I gave him a single-serving size packet of K-Y jelly from the supply closet. "Put this on the tip, first," I said.

The next day he returned with glazed eyes and a smile. He slipped a gram of hash in my upper pocket. "Thanks, man," he said. I nodded. As soon as he left I traded it to the kid in the lab next to mine who did all the blood counts. He gave me a pair of surgical scissors, which I used for clipping pictures out of magazines.

After five months I went to see the parole board. I was very tense because they were going to determine how much of the sixty days to six years I would have to serve. I had already served a hundred and fifty days, so I thought I could advance the argument that I had done enough time, and was ready to go home.

Three parole judges made up the board. There was nothing I could do to prepare except to practice my physical and facial gestures in the mirror. For days ahead of time I practiced looking sorry, levelheaded, bright-eyed, and determined to succeed. I wanted to appear reformed, thoughtful, and eager to enter a crimeless future, and I thought my gestures would amplify my argument for release.

My caseworker at the time, Mr. Wilcox, was preparing to

retire. It was his job to advise me on all prison procedures and generally keep an eye on my progress. But he was slacking off and took no personal interest in me. During my first meeting with him he actually sat back in his chair and fell asleep as I talked about my plans for college. We only met twice after that, and when I asked him questions about my release his response was always "Wait and see." I didn't need him to tell me that.

On the day of my hearing he was supposed to sit with me and tell the judges that I had stayed out of trouble, had a good job, and was a model prisoner. Or something like that. But he was sick that day, so I went in alone.

The panel was made up of two men and a woman, all middle-aged. They were flanked by three guards, for protection. One judge's name was Mr. Dove, which I thought was a good omen, because I kept thinking that I would soon be free as a bird. That was wishful thinking. Once I sat down and crossed my hands on my lap and struck my remorseful, thoughtful, and bright-eyed pose, the woman looked up and asked, "What happened to the ten thousand dollars?"

I gave her a thoughtful look. "I spent it on my lawyer and gave the rest to my father," I said, lying a little. "He needed it."

"Did you pay taxes on it?" she asked.

"No," I replied. "I didn't realize I had to."

As she made a note she said, "Ignorance of the law is no excuse. Not paying taxes is a federal offense."

"Perhaps when I'm released and get a job I can pay the government," I suggested. "I'm willing to do that."

She made a sour face. I looked at the two guys and freshened up my smile. Finally, one said, "Two thousand pounds of hash is one of the biggest hash busts in U.S. history. We'll have to take that into consideration."

"Only a hundred pounds was ever recovered," added the other judge.

"Where's the rest?" the woman asked, with renewed annoyance.

"They sold it," I said.

"Who is 'they'?" she asked.

"The owners," I replied. "Hamilton and Rik. I just worked for them."

"We have no record of that," Mr. Dove said. "We have here that you sailed a boat with one ton of hashish into New York City and sold it. We want to know where the money is."

"I only received ten thousand dollars," I said.

The woman looked up and cocked an eyebrow at me. "That's your side of the story," she said harshly. "The prosecuting attorney claims that you were not very cooperative at the time of your sentencing, and I don't find you terribly cooperative at present."

I didn't know how to respond. I had prepared to be contrite and sincere, not combative. And the few minutes I had to make a good impression were all going to hell, and I could feel my composure unraveling.

"Thank you," Mr. Dove said. "You'll be hearing from us."

I stood up. I felt insane from having absolutely no control over my fate. I left the room and the moment I returned to my cell I worked over my face. Three weeks later I received a letter announcing that I had a two-year setoff until seeing them again. That was hard to take. Two years before I would see them again, and there was nothing I could do but take it.

Others got their setoff letters, too. Soon a guy came up to me in the hallway and said, "Give me a list of all the drug dealers you know, and I'll give you a list of all the ones I know. Then we each can make a deal with the Feds and snitch on the dealers and get out, and then once we are back out on the street no one will know we snitched them out."

"I've been hearing this scam all week," I said. "You are the fifth guy who asked me for a snitch list. You got to come up with some ideas of your own."

This kind of thing happened all the time. One guy got a nutty idea on how to get out and before long every guy in the prison was trying it on every other guy. I avoided them. Their desperation made them all the more dangerous.

Because the skin on my face was so messed up it was difficult to shave properly, so my shaving became an exercise in landscaping—as if I were shaving around flower beds and trees and rocky outcroppings. I could never get a close, even shave. After a while I began to manipulate my face as if I were a makeup artist getting myself ready to be filmed for some role as a psychotic or hardened criminal. There were grooming rules in prison. I wasn't allowed to alter my appearance so radically that it seemed I was preparing to disguise myself and escape. I couldn't do anything permanent like carve "killer" on my forehead and wait for it to scar. No facial tattoos. No head shaving. No beards. But raging acne, mustaches, and elaborate sideburns were acceptable. For a time I looked like an unevenly trimmed topiary, but gradually as I got used to my new life, my skin settled down and I regained my face.

From my cell window I could see a line of houses in the distance. As the months passed, I watched people celebrate their lives—Easter, Memorial Day, Independence Day, Labor Day. In October I watched them put up Halloween decorations. We didn't celebrate Halloween in prison—or, I should say, every day in prison was scarier than any Halloween, so there was no reason to do anything special on October 31st. But thinking of Halloween reminded me of a funny story from when I was in fifth grade. We were living in Kendall, Florida, right on the train tracks. One Halloween afternoon police cars flooded our neighborhood and announced that Halloween was canceled because there had been a prison break upstate at Raford. A couple of guys had hopped a freight and the cops thought they may have jumped off in our area. We locked our doors and turned on all the lights. We pulled the curtains. All night I scampered from window to window peeking out and looking for unshaven suspicious types in striped outfits. Every time a bush rustled in the wind my heart leapt. I saw rugged prison mugs in every shadow. It was the most exciting Halloween ever. The escapees were caught not far from our house and I was disappointed that I hadn't spotted them slinking around.

The memory of my youth was such a surprising relief from all the hatred and despair, blood and drugs that surrounded me. From then on I kept looking out my cell window and from time to time it seemed I could see into my past and amuse myself with stories about my family and old friends. I wrote these stories down in my prison journal, and it gave me a lot of pleasure to recall my childhood.

6 / marking time

I didn't keep a calendar on my wall. I didn't need one. I knew how many days I had been in, and figured in my mind how many days I had left. Like me, a lot of guys kept time in their heads. But everyone had their own system. Most x'd off days on a calendar. Some tallied up numbers like card players: four marks down and one across, like little gates.

One guy I knew took the corner of a razor blade to his arm and made a small cut each day. He wanted the scars to remind him of his pain. I couldn't wait until I got out so I could begin to forget.

One thing I noticed is that guys never told anyone their exact exit date. They just left silently—no parties, no backslapping, no addresses exchanged. They just vanished. It was the safest way to leave. No one wanted some jealous freak or a psycho with a grudge to jump him on the way out.

For me, Sundays were the worst. I counted out the days in units of seven. All my numbers were divided by or multiplied by seven. And every Sunday, when I got to the end of another unit, I was torn between thinking that another week of my life had been lost and that I was one week closer to my exit. In order to make time pass more quickly I got permission to go down to the medical offices, where I cleaned up the X-ray room and the developing room. Mr. Akers, a prison administrator, had me mop and clean his office, too. The floor guard would always unlock Mr. Akers's office for me, and then lock it behind me when I finished. The guard never stayed while I cleaned, but drifted back down the hall to his post.

I was cleaning one Sunday morning when I noticed Mr. Akers had failed to lock the medical file cabinets which held the records for the entire population—and not just medical records, but duplicate paperwork for the main records. I knew my file was in there and I wanted to read it. I opened the office door and looked down the hall. The guard was still at his post, chatting with another guard. I quietly closed the door and dashed to the file cabinet and pulled open the drawer. I fingered across the files until I found mine. I pulled it out. I rechecked the guard. He was still chatting. I opened my file. The parole board report was on top. I read as fast as I could. They called me "uncooperative and unwilling to tell the truth." It was crushing. I felt like screaming. Even though I had fucked up, I wasn't a fuckup, but there was no way I could explain this to anyone. After all, it didn't matter who I was, it was what I had done that now defined me.

I turned the page. The results of my meeting with the psychiatrist were listed. He summarized me as a "situational sociopath willing to give answers that attempted to redefine who he was, rather than to honestly describe himself. Perhaps," the doctor wrote, "he doesn't have the capacity to entirely articulate who he is." That was a fancy way of calling me a liar. I flipped through the rest of the chart. My caseworker, Mr. Wilcox, said I was not a danger to myself or others and ranked me as a minimum-security risk. That was reassuring. I closed the file and checked the door. The guard was still talking. I returned my file to the drawer, closed it, and locked the cabinet.

When I was back in my cell I recorded everything I could remember from my papers, even though most of it was so discouraging. I felt anxious. I tried to shrug it off and read, but couldn't concentrate. I paced around the cell thinking that I was in some kind of reverse mental institution where I'd only get released once I was totally screwed up. I tried to sleep but the anxiety stayed with me.

The next morning it caught up to me. I was tired. I was shaving and staring hard in the mirror, which was warped and gave my face the shape of an unshelled peanut. Suddenly my heart started pounding. My neck swelled with pressure. My ears closed. My eyes glazed over. And I began to think I wouldn't make it out and, like so many guys I had helped sew up, I would take the razor and begin to hack and slice at myself as only a madman would. It wasn't a new thought for me to think I might go insane, but I had always pushed the thought aside. This time the thought that I'd kill myself was unrelenting. As my hand began to shake I knew I was a moment away from hurting myself. I dove toward my cell door as if from the path of a speeding train. I shoved the razor out of the meal slot then dropped down and did push-ups until I couldn't do any more and lay there stretched out on the hard floor feeling the warmth of my body replaced by the cold of the concrete.

By the time the count guard came by I was sitting on my bunk, half shaved and trying to will my shaking foot into a shoe.

Visiting hours were only on weekends and no one ever came to see me anyway so I was surprised when the hospital guard rapped on my door one weekday afternoon and unlocked it.

"You have a visitor," he said. "Two of them."

I had no idea who it might be. I got dressed and followed the guard. We passed through the first set of front gates and entered the visiting room. My father and my uncle Jim from Pennsylvania were sitting on folding metal chairs and smoking cigarettes. The way they were slumped forward made me realize they were drunk.

"Son," Dad said, perking up when I walked in. He stood and lurched toward me. We hugged and I felt myself holding him up. He smelled of hard liquor—Canadian Club. That's what he always turned to when he wanted to get hammered. Uncle Jim grinned. "How're you doing?" he asked. I shrugged.

The guard stepped forward. "I'll give you fifteen minutes," he said, then left the room.

"Goddamned place is closed up tight as a nun," Dad said. "We had to bang on the front door to get someone to open it up."

"It is a prison," I reminded him.

"We would have been here earlier but Jim spotted a roadhouse and we thought we'd have a few belts before coming in. You know, take the edge off of being here." He waved his arm around and stumbled. A chair fell over.

I looked over toward the guard, who was watching through the viewing window.

"Dad, I hate to tell you this, but visiting hours are Saturday. They only called me up here because you came from so far away."

"Well, hell," he said. "Can't a dad visit his son?"

"During regular hours," I said. "Look, I'm going to have to go in a few minutes. Is there anything you wanted to say?"

"Wish I had a drink," he said, and laughed.

I walked over to the guard. "Can he come back in the morning?" I asked.

"Not until the weekend," he replied. "You know the rules."

I went back to my dad. "Can you guys get a motel in town and come back Saturday? We can have the whole day together."

"I got to be getting back home for work," Jim said. "Your dad is up for a visit and we just thought we'd take a crack at running down here and seeing you."

"Well, I'm disappointed," I said. "It would be really nice to have some time to talk."

The guard tapped on the window.

"I got to go," I said. "Thanks for coming." I gave them each a hug. Dad mumbled that he loved me, and I mumbled the same thing back. At that moment we were not so much in love as we were beat up from loving each other.

By the time I returned to my yellow room I was fuming and just wanted to kick something. I was so mad that he had showed up without any thought of when it was all right to arrive, or how it would look to the guards that my dad was some drunken slob beating on the front gate and hollering, "Let me in! I'm here to see my kid!" I could just imagine some report going into my file describing my home life. I felt even more insane.

But by the time I finished writing about it in my journal I had settled down. It was never like my dad to have a lot to talk about anyway, unless he had a good story to share. I'm sure he got drunk just in order to get up the nerve to walk in the door and tell me he loved me, and after that eruption of sentimentality, he wanted out. It was really harder for him than it was for me. It made me think that it must be harder for the visitors to come in than for the prisoners to visit with them. We were used to being inside. And for my dad to see his kid in prison, locked up, it was killing him. Arriving drunk and at the wrong time was the best he could do. And not hurting myself was the best I could do.

After seeing my psychological report I set up another meeting with the shrink. When I settled into the chair in front of his desk I noticed it was bolted to the ground. I had cleaned his office, too, and knew there was an alarm button under his desk he could press for emergency help. A lot of guys didn't like the shrink for the same reason I didn't—he had too much power over our lives. His reports to the parole board could extend your time behind bars. Or he could recommend an early release. Visiting him again was a risk, but I needed to do some damage control.

"Tell me about yourself," he said, once I took my seat.

I wasn't sure where to begin.

"Here's a hint," he said. "Don't talk about your crime."

"What if that's all I've got on my mind?" I asked.

"Then let's start with your family," he said. "I see here that your father came to visit."

"Yeah," I said. "It was great. He's a good father."

"What about your mom?" he asked.

"She's totally supportive," I said. "She's wonderful."

"And your brothers and sister?"

"I love them. I miss them."

"Do you have anything you want to talk about—the stress, or feelings of anger, or remorse?"

"You know," I said, arranging my face into a sincere expression, "I've really worked through all of that hard emotional stuff. I'm just feeling pretty solid right now. Just doing my time, and hoping to get out and get on with meeting the positive goals in my life."

He stared at me for a long time. Longer than normal. Minutes passed. I sat there trying to hold my trustworthy face. I crossed and uncrossed my legs and hands. I breathed deeply. Then not at all. Then too deeply. I was a fake. I was giving him the fake me and he was just going to sit there for as long as it took for the cracks in me to appear. Slowly I lowered my hands and held on to the bottom of the chair as if I were about to topple over.

Then in a very quiet voice he said, "When you really want to be honest with me, come back. I don't think you are a bullshitter. I just don't think you have walked into my office to get help. You are here to con me, and you don't have to con me. You can tell the truth, and I won't hold it against you."

I couldn't look him in the eye. He had seen right through me. My motives were so pathetically obvious. Worse, I was just the same as every other jailhouse con who walked into his office looking to feed him a fake paint-by-numbers home life.

And instead of standing out as something superior, I ended up just being one of the phonies.

I stood up. "I'll try to open up more next time," I said quietly. I left and never went back.

One morning Mr. Bow took me down to the hole, which was a corridor of isolation cells under the hospital wing, when he was doing basic medical rounds. Nobody got sent down there unless they had done something really bad—like get into a fight where someone gets seriously hurt, or try to escape, or assault a guard.

"Help," came a cry from down the hall. "Help me."

We went down and Mr. Bow opened the solid steel cell door. There was a naked guy lying face down on a mattress with the metal part of a broken light bulb up his ass.

"What happened here?" Mr. Bow asked.

"I was lying in bed and the bulb fell out of the ceiling and went up my booty," he whimpered.

The three of us stared up at the empty light fixture.

Bow turned to me. "Go back upstairs and get Dr. Sokel and tell him to bring some tweezers, disinfectant, and suture material. Move it!"

I ran all the way down the corridor. As I ran I wished all the gates would open before me, and I could just keep running, as far away from this place as I could go.

But I couldn't run out of prison. I did what I was told and got the doctor. I helped him gather his supplies, and as he trotted toward the hole to remove a broken light bulb from a grown man's ass, I went back to my cell. There was nothing to do but feel the despair of that moment, until after feeling it over and over I picked up my journal and wrote it down and emptied it out of me. When I reread what I had written it was as if I had cast a spell on myself and the entire experience filled me up again. I just couldn't get away from it. I poured myself into that book, and it poured itself back into me. It was like pouring one glass of water back and forth between two glasses.

For a long time I had known I wanted to write books, but I didn't have any help and I didn't know what I was doing so it took me a while to figure out what I had to write and how to get started. While in prison, it occurred to me that when I lived at Davy's I could never write about something as unsettling as what I had seen in the hole because when I felt something so intense I jumped up and took a walk or ran to a bar where I had a drink poured into me, and another until I was so numb I couldn't pour anything back onto paper. I didn't have the patience to slow down and see that I had plenty of material to write about in high school. I just didn't have the confidence and determination to sit still and nurture it properly. My mistakes, my self-doubt and insecurity got the best of me. Even as I crisscrossed Florida looking for "juicy" subjects, I missed them all. It seemed the harder I chased after a subject, the faster I ran in the wrong direction. Even while living in the Chelsea Hotel while waiting for my sentencing, I spent more time looking into the mirror at my wounded face than I did into my notebook. And the only time I did settle down to write was when I was sitting on the *Beaver* writing in the ship's log. Even then I didn't think I was writing anything of value. At sea I was reading all those great books and ended up thinking I had nothing great to offer in return. But that was untrue.

In prison I got a second chance to realize I did have something to write about. I found plenty of serious subjects. I had plenty of time to write about them and I couldn't get up and run away, or drink, or smoke dope. When I had my fill of serious subjects I began to think about my life before prison, and I found so much more to write about. Prison may have been serious, but from within it, looking out my cell window, I knew life outside prison was more interesting. And as I sat in my yellow cell with my journal on my lap, I understood I had come all the way to prison to realize that what I had in my past was so much richer than what was before me. My struggle as a writer was a lot like my life, I figured. I made up rules for myself and broke them and made others until I got it right.

7 / getting out

Just as every prisoner has a getting-caught story, every prisoner but the lifers and the executed eventually has a getting-
out story. Most of the stories are pretty routine. A man does his
time, keeps his nose clean, doesn't get into trouble, and is released when either his sentence runs out or the parole board
gives him a date. But some of the getting-out stories are escape
stories—mostly attempted-escape stories.

When I was at West Street I saw an escape-attempt straight
out of a Bugs Bunny cartoon. Three guys had ripped bed
sheets into strips and then braided them into a rope. There was
an exercise period on the roof and because it was cold we wore
big army jackets. When it came time for the escape one guy
wound the rope around and around himself and put on the
biggest coat he could find. There was a guard tower on the roof
and a fence. Two other accomplices faked a fight and drew the
guards' attention while the escapee unwound the rope and
threw it up over the fence and down. He tied the end to the

fence pole and climbed up and over. The second escapee climbed up and over. Then the third. But the bed sheets couldn't hold all their weight and snapped. All three of them fell about four stories. None of them died, but they all ended up in the hospital.

I met a young guy named Quentin, who was an okay kid. He always came off tougher than he was. He was being transferred from a minimum-security prison for a court appearance. Some new charges had been filed against him and he was worried. Too worried to go before a judge again. Since he had minimum-security status, he wasn't handcuffed, and as the guard drove past a cornfield Quentin flipped open his door and bailed out. He hit the road, rolled a few times, then hopped up and ran into the field. The guard stopped the car and hollered for him to come back—he promised he wouldn't tell anyone that he had tried to escape. Just come back and all would be forgiven. But Quentin knew the future charges against him were true and he was crashing through the corn and looking for a way out. He came to a farmhouse, forced open a basement window, and hid in the coal bin for two days. On Sunday the farmer and his wife went to church and Quentin went upstairs, found a set of car keys, and took off in a pickup truck. A few days later, as he stepped out of a grocery store, he was picked up. The truck had been spotted and traced. He never changed the plates.

A group of guys started an "astral projection" circle, where they would sit around a card table and concentrate on breaking down all their molecules into subatomic material and drifting through the fences. That was a waste of time. They went nowhere. Other guys would get furloughs and not return—but were eventually caught. Some guys were on work-release and would walk off the job. But they were always caught. It was always something dumb—like they saw a car with the keys in the ignition, or they went into a bar and got loaded and just decided not to return. Nothing remarkable. There were no daring helicopter rescues, no tunnels, no ingenious plans to dress up as a guard and stroll out through the front door.

Most often the escape attempts were straightforward and totally ineffective—they tried to climb the fence. We all knew it was impossible, but desperate cons like the X-ray tech before me tried anyway. The fence was twelve feet high with triple rows of razor wire on the top, and if you made it over that fence there was a second, identical fence to get over, and there were guard towers with snipers, and bloodhounds in their kennels just waiting to sniff you out. But in the dozen or so attempts I saw or heard about, not one man made it over the first fence.

Still, after the parole board set me off, my mind wandered toward escape plans. I imagined the usual plots—a helicopter rescue, a tunnel, a paperwork snafu and mistaken release. Escape became a mental parlor game. And then I stumbled across a plan that would work. I knew a lot of draft dodgers who had spent time hiding out in Canada. I figured I could, too.

After I had received my minimum-security custody rating from my caseworker, Mr. Bow offered to take me out on an evening furlough to a "special motel where you can get your rocks off." All I had to do was have fun and be back by midnight. Cinderella rules.

Only I wouldn't come back. Before going I would raise cash inside by selling medical supplies. I could check flight schedules and make a reservation by using Mr. Bow's office phone when I mopped his floors on the weekend. And once he dropped me off at the motel, I could cab it to the airport, catch a flight to Canada, and be over the border before I was missed. I knew it would work. It was simple. And it was tempting, but being a fugitive for life was too much of a risk.

Yet, it was delicious to imagine.

My real getting-out story was nothing like the one I had imagined. First and foremost, I got a new caseworker. Mr. Wilcox retired, and I was assigned to Mr. Casey. He was young, and not yet beaten down by the brutal atmosphere and the frustration of trying to help people in pretty hopeless situations. So I tried one more long shot. I went to him and told him that I wanted to go to college and that if I got accepted to one while still in prison did he think I could persuade the parole board into giving me an early release to go to school.

"I never heard of an escape plan like that before," he said. "If you get accepted to a school, I'll write a Special Progress Report and we'll give it a try."

That was all the hope I needed to get me fired up. I went down to the library and asked the librarian if they had a Barron's guide to colleges. They didn't. So I went to Mr. Bow's office and asked him to buy me one. I told him I'd pay him back somehow, but for now I just needed the book.

The next day he brought one in. We pored over it. "Okay," I said, "I want to go to a school with a writing program but I don't have any writing. So let's find a school, any school that has low standards, and I'll offer them cash."

We flipped through the pages and found a small school in New York. Graham Junior College. It was a two-year school with a focus on communication arts. Their motto was "Learn by Doing." That sounded fine to me.

I sent away for an application. I had Mr. Casey mail my request from his house so the envelope would not be stamped with U.S. Dept. of Corrections, like all outbound prison mail. I used his address for the return. Soon, they responded. I filled out the application, and in my cover letter I made it extremely clear to them that I was not applying for financial aid—that I was a one-hundred-percent cash-paying student. I figured that would speak louder than my mediocre transcripts from Sunrise High School. I also told them that I would like to enroll as soon as possible—in the mid-year January semester. I spent days crafting my answers to a few short essay questions. My caseworker and I decided since the application didn't ask about arrests or anything like that there was no point in bringing up the subject myself, as it would probably spoil my chances. Mr. Casey typed up the application, wrote a check for the application fee, and sent it back to them.

A few very slow weeks passed and Mr. Casey called me into his office. He had the reply from the college. I ripped the envelope open. I was accepted! I gave it to Mr. Casey. He read it. "Impressive," he said. And he was true to his word. He wrote out a Special Progress Report on my achievements in the prison, he attached a copy of the college acceptance letter, and he sent it to the parole board for consideration.

This was the real college application. I waited. It was nerve-wracking. My face broke out again. Welts. Boils. Acne. Reservoirs of pus and blood. But I left my face alone this time. I did hundreds of sit-ups. I did push-ups. I sweated it out.

Finally Mr. Casey received a report from the parole board.

He ran up to the X-ray room to give me the news. I had a date. December 18th. I was stunned. Nearly fifteen months after my first night at West Street, I would be released. I read the letter over and over. There were conditions. I had to have a stable place to live in New York City, and a job. I had neither, and right away I was nervous. Mr. Casey let me call my father. I explained what I needed. A week later he called Mr. Casey. He knew a guy in St. Croix whose mother had an extra room in an apartment in Little Italy. I could live there and pay her rent. And the same guy had a brother who would give me a job selling Christmas trees until I could find a steady job after the holiday. Casey called in the information to the parole board. My release was approved. And I was given walking papers.

8 / a closed book

On the morning I left I said good-bye to Mr. Bow and Mr. Casey. They had been so helpful. Without them my stay would have been much longer, and my life much different.

I went down to the discharge closet and picked out some clothes. I chose a clean-cut look. No Superfly outfits. No cowboy duds. No black-leather rebel-without-a-cause rags. No fake orange fur. Just a plain pair of dark slacks, a white shirt with a button-down collar, and a jacket with patches on the elbows. I looked like a librarian, and that was fine with me.

In my yellow cell I filled a brown cardboard suitcase with my belongings and carried it down to the discharge officer's station for my final inspection. The guard put my suitcase on a table and flipped it open. He was good at searching things. He had strip-searched me many times. He set aside my two pairs of prison underwear, two pairs of socks, two round-neck white T-shirts, a pair of sneakers, a pair of work boots, gloves, and a wool cap. I also had a drawing pad and colored pencils, a manila envelope with important prison and parole papers, and my copy of *The Brothers Karamazov*.

The guard picked the book up by the spine and tapped it on the table as if he were shaking sand from a shoe. Nothing came out. He flipped open the jacket and saw the prison library seal. "This is a prison copy," he said. "It belongs here." He set it to one side.

I couldn't say anything. The prison seal was stamped in blue ink for both of us to see. My heart was beating wildly. I had to keep that book. My entire identity as a writer was in that book. Everything I had written was squeezed between Dostoyevsky's great lines, as if my words were his discards. But they were all I had.

"It's my favorite book," I said to the guard. "I'll pay for it." I had been given forty dollars in travel money, along with my bus ticket.

"I'd like to sell it to you," he said. "But I can't. It's prison property."

I looked down at my feet and kept my mouth shut. I wondered if he would give it to me if I said it was my journal. Or if, like the ship's log, it would only be used against me, and I'd be marched right back up to my cell and locked in until my sentence expired. I was just so nervous to be this close to the door that I zippered my lip.

I looked up and smiled, and turned away when he threw it in a return bin. I heard it hit with a thud. That journal was the one and only thing I loved about prison. I knew I'd always have my memory, but my heart was in that book.

I was driven to the bus station by a minimum-security con called Pittsburgh. We checked the schedule and my bus was going to be two hours late.

"Can't leave you here," Pittsburgh said. "Town law don't want no cons loitering. Gotta take you back."

It made me sick to my stomach to have to go back. I offered Pittsburgh ten dollars of my forty-dollar travel allowance. He snapped up the ten.

"You're on your own," he said, and sped away.

I sat on a bench and waited, wondering if the discharge guard would discover my journal and read enough of it to send a search team to come and get me.

Once I boarded the bus and we got underway I just looked out the window and watched the country roll by. It was a joy to have a window that moved. It was a joy to have new thoughts. And then I had a funny realization that I really didn't lose my journal entirely. That between the lines of new, free thoughts were compressed the secret memories of my days in prison. That made me feel better.

When I arrived in New York I took a cab from 42nd Street

to Mulberry Street, where Gabe Virgilio's mother lived. She was expecting me. She had food waiting. She showed me to my room, which was small but had a street view. I loved the room, with its old flowered wallpaper and lace doilies on every surface. I put my cheap suitcase on the bed.

"Do you have more luggage?" she asked sweetly.

"No, this is it," I replied.

"Well, with so few things," she said, "you'll need to wash your laundry often. You just give your clothes to me and I'll take care of them for you."

I wanted to kiss her, she was so kind. After I ate too much dinner, and moved some furniture around for her, and took down the trash, I went to meet her other son, who had a job waiting for me. He was just as kind.

And suddenly—in two days—I went from X-raying convicts with broken bodies to selling X-mas trees in Little Italy. And everyone seemed happy. People were nice to me. On the Christmas tree lot we had hot coffee with Sambuca in it, and cookies, and calzones and pizza and pasta and every wonderful food I could want. The good cheer of the holiday season was in everyone. I was in heaven. And I laughed about it. I kept looking around thinking, I've made it. I'm out. I'm out. I'm out. I'm out. And I'd eat some more, and talk to people who came to buy trees, and play with their kids, and I found myself going up to complete strangers and saying, "Can I help you?" instead of imagining that every stranger was a danger.

Part of my job was to deliver the trees to people's apartments. The last job I'd had in New York was pushing a shopping cart full of drugs down the streets to people's apartments. Now I was pushing a shopping cart with a Christmas tree on it. I laughed like a loon at the nutty irony. And when I carried and tugged the trees up three or four or five flights of stairs, I laughed. Nothing could get me down. It was all so comical, and so joyful.

When the January semester began I got my money from Newman and went to school. After his fee and the thousand I gave my father I had just enough to cover the first semester. I paid cash, but I needed spending money, so I got a work-study job at the school. They made me a security guard. At night, I'd walk through the deserted school buildings, checking doors and windows. I had a time clock to punch at various checkpoints on my rounds. Each time I punched my card I shouted, "COUNT!"

In my writing classes, I first wrote brutal stories about prison, about New York street life, about the men I knew who had hard lives and hard hearts. And then one day I got tired of all the blood and guts and hard lives and hard hearts and began to write more stories about my childhood, like the ones I had started writing down in prison—stories which at one time

I did not think were important, but suddenly had become to me the most important stories of all. They contained the hidden days of my innocence and happiness. And once I began retrieving the lost pleasures of my childhood, I began to write stories for children. And I laughed about that, too. Prison certainly wasn't funny, but with each new day it was receding into my past. The mistakes I made, the pain I endured, the time I wasted were now the smallest part of me. But no matter how small, it wouldn't entirely go away. One night I was lying in my bed in Mrs. Virgilio's house, reading, when I glanced up from the book to the ceiling. The naked lightbulb suddenly reminded me of the man with the bulb busted up his ass and I got a surge of anxiety. I hopped up and looked out the window as if the anxiety was tailing me like the Feds had. But no one was down there. I turned and saw my razor on the dresser. I grabbed my shoes and darted out of the room and took a walk.

Every now and again an anxious moment like that comes back, but not often enough to prepare for so I get caught up in it until I shake it off.

I never returned to dig up the hash. I was broke, and exhausted with the heavy schedule between my work and college. I needed money. I could have recovered the hash, cut it into grams and sold it piecemeal, and it would have been worth about five thousand dollars. Once, to be honest, I got as far as the drinking fountain. "Thirty-nine steps, twenty steps, fifteen steps," I said to myself. But my feet wouldn't move. My heart wasn't in it. I would not let myself make that kind of mistake again. No matter how desperate for money I was, I knew giving in would reveal that I was desperate on the inside in an even worse way—and I wasn't, not anymore.

Now, every time I pass the Plaza Hotel and General Sherman, I smile. And once, by chance, I walked by Lucas's old apartment. I didn't stop. Not only would it have been a parole violation to see him, or Hamilton, again, but I didn't want to dig them up either.

I did get the ship's log back. Years later I had Newman request my court records, and the log and files were sent to me. But the *Karamazov* journal is gone. It was the biggest loss of writing I've ever suffered. Since then I've never lost a journal. Now I wonder if that volume is still on the prison library shelf. I hope so. That thought sustains me. I imagine some prisoner checking it out and reading my book within that book. And maybe he will add his thoughts to it, and maybe others will, too. Maybe the library will become filled with books with the trapped world of prisoners' thoughts concealed between the lines.

What remains of the rotted hash is hidden in the hole I dug for it. And I'm out in the open doing what I have always wanted to do. Write.